THE REALITY OF ABUSE,

the Aftermath and the Recovery

"Be Heard, Get Help to Heal"

Dorothy Patterson

The Reality of Abuse, the Aftermath and the Recovery

"Be Heard, Get Help to Heal

Edit by Paul Conant PWC Editing

ISBN 10: 1-68411-521-3
ISBN 13: 978-1-68411-521-1

This book is written to inspire.

Each chapter is loaded with real life issues from both a personal and spiritual viewpoint. This book is so real you will be driven to read with the expectation of revelation, inspiration, and admiration. Buckle up and brace yourself for the real-life drama that I have experienced and gained knowledge and wisdom from. These learning experiences have forced me to open my eyes to accept "The Reality of Abuse, the Aftermath, and the Recovery."

Welcome! May your voice be heard to be helped to heal after reading "The Reality of Abuse, the Aftermath and the Recovery."

Dedicated

To "YOU"!

I pray that as YOU continue to read each chapter, YOU will feel the message of love written in this book especially for YOU. It is my hope that by sharing my turbulent trials and unforeseen triumphs, YOU can avoid some of the pain I have suffered. May God fill YOU with knowledge and enrich YOU with His infinite wisdom. God allows us to go through things in life to strengthen us in love, peace and understanding. YOU are the sole purpose for this book. I ask God, our Father **(the finisher of all things)** that by the time YOU finish the last chapter, YOU will undoubtedly have some of the "WHY ME" questions answered

Preface

How long will you walk in the shadow of reality? At the age of twenty, this was all I could ask myself as I paced back and forth.

Now as a woman, the lies that have shaped my life are no one else's blame but mine. Each day had become not only a fight, but a struggle to overcome the darkness of pain I had grown accustomed to living within. I was ashamed of myself because I knew I was comfortable with being uncomfortable. The scars from my childhood continued to haunt and taunt me, never leaving a moment of peace.

If my sisters knew about playing house they should have warned me not to "play house" with Daddy. No matter how hard I tried, I could not escape the visions of me playing the secret game of house. The images of my frail tender little body being laid down to be explored and abused, to this day at times my body grips with fear, feeling as though it was still happening, at the hands of my stepfather, the only man I knew and loved; he was my Daddy.

Acknowledgements

To my Lord and Redeemer, the Giver of insightful ability to understand the difference between wisdom and knowledge. (Pro. 8:11 KJV: "For wisdom is more precious than rubies, and nothing you desire can compare with her.")

To my angels, my sons Dralon and DeMarcus, who strengthened me through my struggles;

To my sisters and friends who believed in me when I did not or could not believe;

To my only brother James, no matter what you hear or believe, I forgive you. Now forgive yourself. "I love you still and always!"

To Mr. Gray for keeping me encouraged.

Special Thanks

To my mother for shaping me into the woman I am today. You <u>showed</u> me "NO matter the odds, never ever stop trying or fighting!"

To Mr. Paul: you are one man that I respect highly. Your words of wisdom, correction, and guidance have helped me express myself better; even when we did not agree.

And last but not least, thanks to those of you who held me accountable and valued my opinion about life!

I love and appreciate each of you very much!

TABLE OF CONTENTS

Introduction

B efore my Daddy taught me how to "play house," he was my best friend. Anytime I needed him he was there. He played with me when Mommy was too tired to play. Every time he would leave to go to work or church I would be so sad until he came back home. Yes, my Daddy was the pastor of the church.

Reflecting back, I can still see myself beaming with pride as I watched my Daddy put on his long white robe he wore on Sundays. He would grab his Bible; take my hand, and say, "You ready to say Amen?"

I bobbed my head up and down, saying "yes," and giving him the big smile he always loved to see on my face.

Daddy would go to the pulpit and I would go sit on the front row in order to make sure he could hear me say "Amen," just in case no one else did.

Getting the church to say "Amen" was never a problem for my Daddy because his members loved the way he preached the gospel.

I loved the way Daddy strolled from one end of the pulpit to the other as he shouted: "God is good all the time and all the time God is good." Then he would say, "If you know that God has been good to you, stand up and give God some praise!" Everybody would stand up, jumping and shouting, "Hallelujah!" "Praise the Lord!" "Thank you Jesus!" "Glory to your name!" or whatever the Lord has laid on their heart to say.

Once everyone sat back down, the choir would sing a song. Once the choir finished singing the welcoming of visitors was given, then the announcements followed the offering. This was another part of my favorite time at church because I was the only little one who could quote the Scripture Daddy said every Sunday before the offering, word for word.

The musician softly played the offering song, "You Can't Beat God's Giving."

We would all stand up while Daddy read the Scripture. I'd say it right along with Daddy quietly: "[8]Will a man rob God? Yet ye have robbed me. But ye say, Wherein have we robbed thee? In tithes and offerings. [9]Ye are cursed with a curse: for ye have robbed me, even this whole nation. [10]Bring ye all the tithes into the storehouse, that there may be meat in mine house, and prove me now herewith, saith the LORD of hosts, if I will not open you the windows of heaven, and pour you out a blessing, that there shall not be room enough to receive it."

As soon as he finished, he would shout: "I just read to you Malachi 3: 8–10. It's offering time!" The choir sang while everyone marched around the offering table to give according to how God had blessed their life. After the offering, the choir would sing one more song, and then Daddy would get up to preach the Word of God. I enjoyed watching Daddy preach. He knew exactly what to say to get the congregation to clap their hands, shout "Preach pastor," and "Amen." As soon as Daddy dismissed the service I would run up to him and say what I heard all the other members say: "You really let the Lord use you today."

Daddy would just laugh, saying, "Yes, He did." My fond memories of my Daddy, the pastor of the church, soon ended. It all started or at least as far back as I can remember when I was five. The innocent child in me wanted to believe my Daddy was a man of God. He wouldn't do anything that would not please God.

Therefore, I convinced myself to accept that what my Daddy started doing to me was okay. When he brought me my "special gifts," I always sat on his lap where the bump in his pants was and give him a big kiss on the cheek! This was our routine for a long time.

When I started school, Daddy stopped giving me gifts; instead he said, "Hugs and kisses are better than gifts." Since Daddy was my best friend, I had no problems giving my daddy hugs and kisses all the time without getting a gift. The real changes between Daddy and me started when he asked me to rub his shoulders. He said they were sore from him working so hard at work. I eagerly rushed into the house every day after school so I could rub Daddy's shoulders to make him feel better.

I remember like it was yesterday: Daddy picking me up from school and taking me to M.E. Moses, my all-time favorite store because all my favorite candies were there. Jumping with joy as I got out of the car, I asked: "Daddy, do I get to pick my own candy?" He replied, "Yes, and you can pick fifty cents worth. "Wow!" I said, jumping with joy.

This was the first time I was allowed to get more than twenty-five cents worth of candy. As I began to pick my candy, I wondered why. I asked Daddy, "Is this a special day for me?"

He picked me up, whispering in my ear, "Yes, today is a special day for you."

I remember vividly looking puzzled because it was not my birthday and I didn't get my report card so why was today special?

Daddy knew I was confused so he said: "Today is special because I'm going to play house with you."

"Yippee!" I shouted. Because I had asked Daddy so many times to play house with me and he would always say, "Not today, maybe tomorrow."

When we got home Daddy did just as he promised—he played house with me. I had so much fun playing with Daddy. We played house every day. This was so much fun in the beginning, but I was starting to get tired of playing.

Daddy must have sensed I was getting tired, so he told me we were going to play in the bed this time. This didn't bother me because I trusted my Daddy.

Before we got in the bed, Daddy made me promise not to tell Mommy. Whispering in my ear, "This is our little secret," as he rubbed his hands all over my little body. Daddy looked different to me and for the first time I was scared of my Daddy, my best friend. Daddy must have seen the fear in my eyes as he began to put his hand in my pants, so he stopped.

We played house so much it became my after-school routine, and since Daddy rubbed all over me every time it didn't even bother me anymore, and I never said anything to Mommy about it. Besides, Daddy told me she would never believe me, and he was right, because every time Mommy got ready to leave me with Daddy, no matter how much I begged to go with her, she always said, "Daddy will take good care of you."

I wanted to scream, "Mommy, Daddy is touching me wrong! He's touching me in the places you said no one was to touch but you or my sister's only while giving me a bath," but

I didn't because just like Daddy said, she would not believe me anyway. I remember it like it was just yesterday, when Daddy told me we were going to play house differently today. The reason I can remember it so well is because it was the day I had lost my front tooth and the tooth fairy left me a quarter under my pillow for my tooth. Excited about the money I had gotten for my tooth, Daddy said he would take me to the candy store and let me spend the money I got from the tooth fairy. I was even more excited because I would not have to play house with Daddy. My excitement left as soon as we got back home from the store because the bed was not made. I knew exactly what that meant. Without delay, I did my normal routine of getting in the bed lying on my back, and waited for Daddy to start rubbing all over me. To my surprise, Daddy didn't do the rubbing as long as he had done all the other times, which was unusual for Daddy. It wasn't long before I found out why Daddy didn't rub all over me for long.

This was the first of many times his hands found their way to Agnes (This is what Mommy called the woman's anatomy). I can at times still feel his hands rubbing all over me as his fingers found their way to Agnes. He parted my legs, put Vaseline on his fingers and began to try to put them inside Agnes.

It didn't feel good, it hurt, but he told me "it will only hurt for a little while, but you will get used to it". I was so innocent. I trusted him even though I knew what he was doing was wrong. Daddy slowly worked his finger inside of me for some time and he was right—it stopped hurting me. By the time I was eight, Daddy could put two fingers inside me without it hurting. This was once again his daily after-school routine for me. So without having to be told, I made my way to their bedroom like it was the norm for an eight-year-old child to be doing this.

By the time I reached the age of nine, Daddy was fully raping me. He would play with Agnes for a little while and then he would slowly part my legs and climb on top of me and place his oversized manhood inside of me. Although he could not completely get himself inside me, it still hurt each time no matter how much Vaseline he used.

The only way I got Daddy to stop was to tell him a lie. Before my twelfth birthday, I told Daddy that I had started my period just so he would stop raping me. The idea came when I overheard my older sisters talking about their menstrual cycle and how they had to make sure to stay away from boys because they didn't want to have a baby. Once Daddy heard this he instantly stopped raping me.

However, he still used his fingers on me to pleasure himself, which was a welcomed relief because I had gotten used to him, his fingers and the Vaseline. It wasn't until about a year later when Daddy finally grew tired of me. I guess he decided to end pleasuring himself using me because people were starting to comment about how quickly my breast and behind were developing. Whatever the case may have been, I was glad he stopped messing with me.

Chapter 1
My Fairytale Is Over

What a horrific experience for me as a child not only to endure, but be forced to live as though my life at home was perfect. To outsiders, I could understand why my life could appear to be perfect because for black people to live the way we did in a small town in the early 80's was a rarity. We lived in what some would call a mansion on the hill. Our multi-level home sat on three acres of land encompassed by a circular driveway, which led up to the two-and-a-half car garage. Parked on the inside of the garage was my stepfather's "Purple Good Time Van" with plush seats, television, and a small kitchenette inside. It was extremely nice. My mom's limited-edition yellow Mark V with electric-heated seats, dual cassette player, and power-operated windows sat just on the other side. Once those who came to visit got over the shock of the van and the limited-edition Mark V, I understood why my life to those on the outside would seem perfect, because no one else in town had a van or car like my parents.

My life had all the makings of prestige. Besides the house and cars, I had the designer clothes and shoes to emulate the lifestyle of the rich and famous.

My designer wardrobe consisted of Calvin Klein, Izod, Gloria Vanderbilt, and my favorite of all the designers, Ralph Lauren. My designer shoes consisted of Kaepa, Converse and K-Swiss sneakers. All designer dress shoes came from Margo's, Sanger Harris, or Joske's.

When I reflect back on my high school years, I still laugh at myself. I thought I was the best thing walking, especially since I knew that many of my classmates waited with anticipation for me to get to school just to see what I was wearing. They all knew that it was going to be something that they had not seen in any store around town.

Because I was dressed to impress all the time, I had to have the grades to match. I still to this day remember how obsessed I became with my academic performance my senior year. I had to make the honor role at the end of every six weeks. Even though I goofed off a lot, I still kept my GPA at a 3.8.

Not only were my academics on point but also I was a gifted athlete. I played basketball and ran track. In basketball, I had to get a triple or a double in every game. For those of you who do not know what that means, I will explain. When you rebound and score during the game that is a double. When you rebound, score, and steal the ball during the game that's a triple. Being known for my quickness, I was sure to get at least two steals, twelve points, and six to seven rebounds per game. I was the star of the game. Well, almost the star. I had one teammate who outscored me all the time, but she couldn't touch me when it came to rebounding or stealing the ball in a game. However, my excitement from having a good game left as soon as I would turn and look into the cheering crowd only to see no one from my family there to cheer for me. Due to the house I lived in, my designer clothes and my athletic abilities, I became the star of my own fairytale, "My Perfect Life."

My stardom came with a cost. It made me the envy of my associates, friends, enemies and some of my family members. Blinded with envy, they could not see the torment in my eyes or the frown behind my smile. I laughed when nothing was funny, smiled when I should have been crying and cried when I should have been laughing. My life was chaotically raw and real!

The roughness of my life: I was scarred deeply by the hands of the man I knew as Daddy. He had my pride and self-worth in his hands and the innocence of my childhood. He took the most precious gift God gave me as a woman, my virginity.

I have spent many years wondering what my life would have been like if I had been given the opportunity to give my virginity to the man of my choice. Due to my inability to cope with the hand I had been dealt, I allowed lies to be my healing ointment and a fairytale lifestyle to be the Band-Aid to cover my scars I hid inside my heart.

I have had many physical scars heal in weeks, but the mental scars have taken years to heal.

I came to the realization that the only way for me to escape the mental madness was to open up my heart to the raw but real truth that I was a victim as a child, not as a woman. As a woman, I could not allow myself to spend the rest of my adult life having a pity party as a victim. I had to tell myself over and over I would no longer allow the abuse I endured to keep me locked in the mindset of a victim. All the fairy- tales I had read as a child were just that—books of make believe. "PATTIE CAKES ain't pattin' anymore; LONDON'S BRIDGE ain't falling down—it's done fell down; CINDERELLA still ain't got her fellow; and "SNOW WHITE's" prince is still a frog. ALICE ain't wondering no more, and all THREE of the LITTLE PIGS got smart enough to build brick houses. Raw but Real: the reality of abuse is real, the aftermath is chaos, but the recovery from abuse and the aftermath of being abused is possible once you rid your mind of the fairytales: "MY FAIRY TALE IS OVER!!!!!!!"

Chapter 2
Reality

"REALITY" was the one thing I had problems with for many years: The fantasies in my mind were easier to accept.

I couldn't bring my heart to believe that the people who were supposed to cherish, protect, and love me could overlook, excuse, or ignore the pain they caused in order to appear faultless and perfect. Throughout my childhood, I was told, "Children were to be seen and not heard" and "Whatever goes on in our house stays in our house." This is why I buried my pain and the real truth about what was going on in the perfect house on the hill.

While growing up, the pure and sincere love I gave to those closest to me was only returned when they stood to gain or expect something from me in return. In order to receive love or feel accepted I had to always sacrifice my feelings. I wanted nothing more than to be loved with the same pure and sincere love I gave out. So I mastered hiding my true feelings.

In order to maintain my sanity, I spent countless years lying, being deceitful, and pretending. I felt I had to do these things to appear normal in a world where I was surrounded by conditional love. Waking up most mornings not remembering which lie I had told or who I told the lie to caused my head to have a constant ache. The headaches had to stop, and the only way to stop them was to release the burning truth within me. I could not continue the way I was living. I had to surrender and accept "REALITY."

My fear of not being loved became the driving force of my self-sacrificing behaviors. I did not want to continue to sacrifice myself, but I didn't know how to stop. I knew I needed to change, but something within me would not allow me to do things differently. Therefore, I continued pretending, ignoring my heartfelt emotions, and sinking deeper into my delusional world, which left me empty and incomplete.

I rushed into marriage because I was pregnant at eighteen and determined not to let my child be labeled a bastard. Once married, I had another son and began trying to follow the footsteps of Ward and June Cleaver's "Leave It to Beaver": the ideal family I grew up watching every day. The Cleavers lived the American Dream: "Big house; tall, handsome husband; sophisticated wife; two beautiful sons; and a happy dog."

After I married I thought my life was meaningful because I, too, like the Cleavers had a tall, handsome husband, was a sophisticated wife, had two beautiful sons, and a happy dog we named Roscoe.

Life for me during this time was based on what my family thought of me and on maintaining the upper-class lifestyle I grew up living.

Absolutely everything from my house, the community I lived in, the cars we owned, and the friend(s) I chose had me right on target with the elite members of society. My wonderful world was established and (REALITY) was nowhere to be found. Not having any concept of (REALITY), I found myself in the darkness of self-pity, hopelessness, anger, depression, despair, and desperation.

Still determined to live in the shadow of (REALITY), I continued to smile and laugh, when I knew deep down inside, I wanted to cry or needed to be crying. Overwhelmed, I went to the bathroom and stood in front of the mirror. Tears began to flow; no longer able to hold them back, I stood there and took an inventory of myself. After what seemed to be an eternity I had to face my childhood, and I came to the conclusion my life was Raw but Real!!!!!!!!!!!!!!!! Emotionally drained and angry with God, I asked: "Why did my life have to be so raw? I invested so much time and money trying to erase my past by creating the perfect life and lifestyle!" Tired of it all, I lost it, screaming as loud as I could: "No more, No more!" Pulling myself together, I said, "You are no longer a child who was to be seen and not heard, but a woman who should be seen and will be heard."

It was at this point in my life I told myself: *"No more lies; I will accept (REALITY) by opening my eyes to see, my ears to hear, and my heart to God, letting God lead me instead of lies, society, family, and friends."*

In a desperate attempt to make sense of my life, I found myself at a motivational seminar.

When the speaker got up she asked, "What is it that you would love to do all day for free?"

I thought, *"What a question!"* My heart started pounding, full of excitement and fear at the same time.

The one thing I would love to do is to share my life experiences with others. I'm praying that it would help them avoid some of the pain I have endured. I was renewed in my mind and spirit after leaving the seminar. I allowed God into my heart. By doing so, God has given me the courage to write this book.

The chapters in this book are packed with real issues and experiences that I pray you will find helpful.

I remember when I was in my teens, my mother would always say: "Ain't no lesson like a bought lesson."

I hope while reading this book, some of the lessons I have paid for can be utilized to ease some of your pain. I am by no means a psychologist or a doctor. However, life has taught me that education does not compare to personal experiences. Textbook theory gives you the knowledge of understanding life's circumstances. Experience gives you the wisdom needed to survive the circumstances of life.

Included are biblical Scriptures that I found very helpful as I accepted my Raw but Real life.

Words of Wisdom from EXPERIENCE!!!!!!

Life at times can be unfair, but if you get to the root of the problems in your life, you will live fairly. If not, the Devil is very crafty and will lead you into self-destructive behaviors which will annihilate you!

Chapter 3
"Reality"-Addicted to Love

"Time to get my party on," I said while taking a sip of my sister's drink. "Dang sis, this drink is strong! What's in it?"

She ran over to me and snatched her drink out of my hand.

"You're not supposed to be drinking!"

"Whatever!" I said as I walked away from her.

Practicing my dance moves I said "We're going to have so much fun tonight!"

The two amigos, my sister and I, were hittin' up the club.

"When we get there, I'm not leaving without my Knight in shining armor," I told myself, with pure confidence resting my hand on my hip and workin' my neck.

I knew I had it goin' on!

I was fifteen when I started using my older sister's I.D. to get into the club.

Without makeup, I looked fifteen, but with it, I looked every bit of twenty.

Giving myself the once over, I thought: *"There's no way the bouncer could deny me access. I had it all: Pretty face, bangin' body, and a designer outfit."*

I wore my black, short, lambskin-leather skirt that fit my hourglass figure (tighter than a bunion sticking out the side of a cheap shoe), with a white butterfly button-down shirt pressed to perfection, finishing it off with a cream, mid-waist, leather jacket. To complete the package, I rocked my sister's cream, Italian, thigh-high leather boots, adding three inches to my height. My 5-foot 7-inch frame turned into a 5-foot-10 towering brick house.

It was ten-thirty when we finally got inside the club. The bouncer just kept looking at me, then back at my sister's I.D. After looking at it three times, he let me enter.

"Man, the music is bumpin' in here."

We went straight to the dance floor, not stopping until the D.J. slowed the music down.

"My goodness, it's hot in here!"

I needed to get to the ladies' room to cool off and to make sure my makeup was still intact. I told that to my sister.

She was happy to go. She needed to wipe her face because it was shinin' like a brand new nickel fresh off the press.

I took one look in the mirror and laughed.

My sister asked me what was so funny.

I told her I had the nerve to think she was the only one shinin'.

She laughed hard because I was shinin' better than a pair of Stacy Adam's spit-shined shoes.

We quickly freshened up our makeup, ready to dance until the lights came on and the D.J. said *"Y'all ain't got to go home, but y'all got to get the Hell outta here!"*

I rushed to exit the ladies' room ahead of everybody because I wanted to be the first one seen by the men who stood around the door, like leaping frogs with their mouths open ready to catch a fly. Since I was not leaving without my knight, I was the fly ready for landing.

When I opened the door there, there was my knight, standing just inches from the dance floor.

As I walked past him, our eyes locked, and he asked me to dance.

I fell in love while we danced to Midnight Star's "Slow Jam."

My knight in shining armor had finally come!

My premature step into womanhood was my downfall. I lost myself within my knight.

I gave him complete control over me. I knew nothing about being a woman, but of course, my knight knew everything.

I fell into an addiction: I was hopelessly addicted to love!

I was naïve to truly believe that in order for someone to be an addict with an addiction, a crack pipe must be used. "REALITY" taught me that a crack pipe is the pipeline a crack addict uses, but there are many pipelines of addiction.

As I said before, "I was hopelessly addicted." Take note of the word "WAS.". In order for me to break the vicious cycle of addiction, I first had to fall in love with myself.

Although your addiction may not be love, anytime you allow a person, place, or thing to take your value, you lose your self-worth.

Loving yourself more than your addiction is the key component needed to have a successful recovery.

For years, I thought I loved myself more than anything, until I met my knight in shining armor.

The more I saw my knight, the more I could not see me. The more my love for him grew, the less I loved myself.

You may not understand how this could happen.

Trust me when I tell you it can happen, easier than you may think. How could I not fall in love with someone who's always available? If I asked, I received.

The more I asked, the more I received.

I was on cloud -nine in la-la land, I became so high on my knight I left the clouds and thought I had found Heaven on earth.

My knight became everything. He seemed to become the air I breathed. No one could get in the way of my love for him. I was so into him, I married him. He became my god. I forgot about God. I tuned out my mother, thinking she was just old fashioned. She did not know him as I did. Besides, she did not even know her own husband, so how can she tell me about my husband.

Friends were just jealous because they could not get a knight like mine.

I mean, I got so wrapped up in my knight, I became blind to the facts that a husband does not stay out all night, or cheat on his wife with other women. Nor does a husband take money from his own household to spend on the women he has on the side. He was doing everything right in front of me. Love had me completely blind. I could not see anything or anyone, beyond my knight. My knight was the only light I needed. Reality of abuse is when you love someone so much it becomes an addiction, before you know it; this addiction totally makes you lose yourself. It causes you to close your eyes to what is real. You become blind and oblivious to what is happening with you and to you. You see light only through the eyes of filtered love. Being addicted to love takes you to people you would have never met, places you would have never seen, and things you would have never had or touched. Simply put, being addicted to love makes you become who you are not.

Allowing yourself to love someone, some place, or something so deeply, you begin to live your life through that love. You begin to love someone, some place, or something more than you love yourself. You completely turn your back to being independent and become co-dependent; that is the worst thing that can happen to a person. You base your happiness in life according to how the love of your life feels.

Speaking from my own experience, I became reckless.

I let the love for my knight get in the way of my ability to love myself.

This left me devoid of survival skills. I knew how to survive only if my knight was happy. No happiness for my knight meant there was very little or no happiness for me.

My life turned into a sea of self-destruction and self-endangerment.

I had lost the little love I had for myself. Devoid of "REALITY" and self-love, I had no common sense to eat or to

43

sleep without my knight. I ate when he ate, I slept when he slept, I forgot all my survival skills; I fell into complete destructive behavior.

I was left without any emotions. How could I survive?

I was trapped and imprisoned because I was an addict of love.

Survival at this point was not for me, only for my knight and children. The person I knew I should be was completely lost. I had to find myself somehow, but I did not know how. I was adrift in a sea of chaos with no compass to find my way back to the shore.

Just as I was about to give up, the pain of "REALITY" began to surface. I began the slow and painful way towards the acceptance of "REALITY"which led me to my recovery.

Although my knight still meant everything to me, I had begun to see that he did not care about the pain he was causing me. He was living the life of a king. He had a great wife at home taking good care of his children, doting on his every need. What more could a man ask for or desire? It seemed the more I tried to please him, the worse he became. Nothing slowed him down. My crying had no effect on his calloused heart.

When I complained, it gave him the perfect excuse he needed to stay away from home. He was never going to change as long as I stayed the same. He was going to continue treating me as if I was nothing more than the servant I had allowed myself to become.

"REALITY" was one hard pill to swallow, but I had to take a deep breath and swallow it to save my sanity.

It was time to stand face-to-face with "REALITY."

After being alone on too many nights, I came to the painful realization that my love was not enough for my knight. I was allowing him to be my pathway to destruction.

I needed inner peace, not more happiness. Where there is no peace, there is war. I was at war with "REALITY." This was a battlefield I should have avoided. I was already lost. My sanity was at stake; I had no energy left to fight.

Still holding on to hope in a hopeless situation, I began to ask myself questions.

Could he love or hold me when I was afraid? No! He was too busy holding other women.

Would he stay and take care of me if I became terminally ill? No! He had too many other women he cared for more than me.

Taking a deep breath, I accepted without any doubt the fairytale was over.

After accepting this I grew spiritually, physically, and mentally. Through my growth and recovery, I learned that loving myself enabled me to face my past pains and fears, giving me the courage to forgive myself for being afraid to let go of my knight and the fairytales of childhood.

I can now say to you, if you are still addicted, realize and accept this: Anyone or anything that has more value to you than your own self-worth should not become the love of your life.

I'm not saying you cannot love someone or something just as much as you love yourself. I am simply saying you should not love anyone or anything **more** than you love yourself. If you find yourself in this predicament, accept the "REALITY" of your situation. If you do not, you will be forced to find another outlet.

Outlets are the plugs used to release pain in order to escape fear. These outlets are even more addictive, giving a false sense of security.

Whatever outlet you plug into, if they are not healthy, they will penetrate their way into your mind, making you believe that destructive behaviors are valuable, leaving you feeling worthless.

When you value something worthless, it becomes your main focus, leaving very little room for "REALITY."

Where there is no "REALITY," the probability of a life of an addict will become all you are worth.

I know it is hard to survive when you have totally lost yourself to an addiction. Addiction can be defeated by the use of willpower.

From experience, I know addiction is hardest to recognize when you have no idea you are an addict.

The only way I realized I was an addict or addicted to love was the night I left my three–month-old baby boy home alone at one-thirty in the morning to look for my knight. As I was walking down the sidewalk full of hurt and disgust for my knight, I said to myself, *"This is insane. I am out walking in the middle of the night looking for someone who obviously is not looking for me, nor is he concerned about our child."*

This was truly the start of my breaking point and true recovery. I may not have had self-love, but I loved my child more than I loved my knight, his father. It snapped me into "REALITY." I revisited my childhood and thought of how hurt I was when my mother put a man, my abuser, before me.

When you have an addiction, you can lie to yourself without guilt as long as you are getting your fix.

The lie the devil tried to use to keep me addicted was when I told myself it was okay to put my knight before my child because my knight was my child's biological father. I still would be better than my own mother because my abuser was not my real father.

My addiction could have cost me my child. The pain from my past and the deep love for my child gave me the willpower to return home and not allow my addiction to control me.

After many years of gathering knowledge, I gained wisdom through experience, which is now my "REALITY."

This experience helped me understand and accept that my knight was not the right one for me.

I am no longer addicted to love. I am addicted to "REALITY." True recovery for me was to understand that without God I was nothing but with God I am conqueror. (Romans 8:37-39: "Nay, in all these things we are more than conquerors through him that loved us. 38 For I am persuaded, that neither death, nor life, nor angels, nor principalities, nor powers, nor things present, nor things to come, 39 nor height, nor depth, nor any other creature, shall be able to separate us from the love of God, which is in Christ Jesus our Lord.")

Getting addicted to this Scripture has taken me on a high that I never want to stop enjoying. It is the high that continues to take me higher.

"REALITY" gives you the ability to use the power of knowledge to fight your addiction and the willpower of wisdom to defeat it.

The easiest way to free yourself from addiction is to **revisit** your past, no matter how painful.

It is vital that you understand why I chose to use the word **revisit**.

More often than not, we have a tendency to continually **relive** our past.

Living in the past is the spark that leads to addiction which jump-starts you into becoming an addict. Put the spark out by **revisiting** your past, not **reliving** the past.

My final point, "When you get weak, concentrate on this thought: **Don't allow the pain of your past to be the reason you live or who you become while living....**"

Chapter 4
Associate, Friend, or Enemy

"Oh God, this cannot be happening!" How could my best friend sleep with my husband? She knows he's my knight in shining armor. I've shared our most intimate secrets with her! We are so close I tell her everything! She watches my kids while I'm at work. I watch her kids while she goes to the club. I just can't believe she would betray me! I was there for her when she lost her house. I endured sitting in the courtroom with her while her only brother got sentenced to prison for ninety-nine years for molesting a child.

Did she not understand how hard it was for me to sit there and listen to the gory details? It was like reliving my own horrible childhood. I sacrificed my feelings and emotions even when she asked me about his case. I did things for her behind my husband's back. I can still remember how mad he would get when he found out I had done something for her. He constantly told me, "She is not your friend." Now I understand why. They were having an affair right under my nose! How could they hurt me like this? They both knew what I had been through, as a child with my family. They were all I had left, other than my kids.

As the tears burned my eyes, I looked up and asked, "Why God, why? How could you allow this to happen? The only two true friends I had and look what YOU let them do to me! How am I supposed to trust you and you continue to let everyone around me betray me?"

The pain I felt in the pit of my stomach burned so bad that I threw up in the hallway trying to make it to the bathroom.

I could not stop the tears from flowing. My heart was broken. How could I mend my broken heart? My best friend, my blood sister, had shattered it!

What was I going to do?

I couldn't divorce him because of my boys. I will not jeopardize their opportunity to be raised in a home with both their parents.

At least this is what I told myself, but the truth was I was too afraid to let my boys be around another man because of what happened to me.

Therefore, I stayed in my marriage for the sake of my boys' emotional and physical health. Again, the self-sacrificing behavior reared its ugly head. Giving very little thought about the disrespect my husband and my sister a/k/a "best friends," had shown me, I remained. This proved to be something I could no longer endure. The thought and fear of him having an affair with my sister took its toll on me.

I found out that on top of an affair with my sister, he was sleeping with several other women. Still not willing to throw in the towel, I stayed with him in the hope that I could love him enough to change him.

My self-sacrificing behaviors continued.

One day when I came home from working, my youngest son said: "Mommy, why do you stay with my daddy when all he does is talk to girls at the swimming pool while you are at work?"

I was not only stunned, but speechless.

What explanation could I give for being a fool?

How could I pretend not to know what was going on? If my eight-year-old son didn't bat an eye at "REALITY," accepting it without hesitation, why couldn't I face "REALITY?"

My only response to him was, "Mommy is working on changing things."

I hoped he would accept the only answer my aching heart could utter.

Right before he was about to enter into his room, he turned and said: "Mommy, you've always taught us to love ourselves, and when someone is doing us wrong, get away from that person. Isn't Daddy doing you wrong by talking to the girls at the pool?"

"Just because Daddy is talking to the girls at the pool doesn't mean he's doing anything wrong," I said as well as I could without showing my true emotions.

"Daddy is doing you wrong, Mommy, because I see him hugging and touching one girl the same way he hugs and touches you."

"Well, in that case, Daddy is doing me wrong. I promise you I will change things."

"Yes!" he said, while jumping up and down, heading to his room.

Tears welled up in my eyes as the pain of "REALITY" entered into my heart.

How can I stay in this marriage and expect my boys to respect me?

The more I sat there thinking about my situation, the madder I got. I had to accept the fact. It's not about me anymore. He has taken his disrespectful ways too far this time.

As if sleeping with my sister wasn't enough, now he was flaunting his infidelity in front of my kids. Enough is enough!

Gathering my composure and what little respect I had left, I made up my heart, not my mind. (The mind can change without God; with God the heart is forever changed.) I was taking the boys and leaving him.

Two weeks later, my boys and I were in our new home.

After ten long years of marriage, my addiction to my "Knight in Shining Armor" was over. Our divorce became final one year later.

My sister, on the other hand, was a totally different situation. How could I not talk to or see her? My mother told us repeatedly while we were growing up: "If you don't have a friend in the world, you have your sisters."

The burdens from my childhood and the pain of losing both my best friends, was too much for me to handle.

The only person I knew that could make sense out of my situation was my mother.

I told her about the situation and she asked me to stay calm until she had a chance to talk to my sister. I agreed because I didn't have the energy to argue or fight.

Mom was about to get up to go talk to her, but I stopped her right before she got up. "I have something else to tell you."

She looked at me puzzled; I'm sure she was "wondering what now?"

I didn't know how to say it, so I just blurted out, "He molested me!"

"Girl, what are you talking about? Who is he?"

With her looking at me square in the eye, hoping she heard me wrong, I answered: "Your husband did," with no hesitation.

"You listen to me," she said: "I will not have you talking about your daddy like this. He is a man of God and would never do anything against God. Do you hear what I'm saying?" She said it in a low and controlled voice.

I sat there at a loss for words. Here I was, sitting with my mother, not only needing to be comforted, but also consoled. The disappointment I felt was overwhelming.

I could not believe she was sitting in front of me defending him.

At this moment all I could hear was him saying, "She will never believe you over me."

I spent years waiting, hoping for this day, hoping to make a liar out of him.

She was supposed to love me more than anything: she's my mother! And she had the nerve to sit there telling me not to speak about her husband. The man wasn't even my real father!

I could not believe it!

"Do you hear me?" She yelled this time.

Pissed and hurt, I yelled, "Yes, he did, and he is going to burn in Hell, too!"

Mama looked like she could kill me, and I thought she would because she was madder than a raging bull chasing a Matador.

She stared at me long and hard.

I truly thought she was about to break down and say she was sorry for not protecting me.

However, she shocked the "Hell" out of me when she said: "The Bible says to forgive and forget."

If a fly was looking for somewhere to land, my mouth was open, wide and available.

How could I forget what had happened to me?

I could not believe she was serious, but the next words that came out of her mouth became the straw that broke the camel's back!

She calmed down and asked me if my seven-year-old son was her husband's?

There is NO word in the dictionary to describe neither my pain nor my anger.

I looked her straight in the eye and said: "You mean to tell me you knew that your husband was raping me and you stayed with him?

"How in the h* could you sleep in the same bed with someone you thought had a baby by your daughter? That's why you could sit in the courtroom and hear your only son get sentenced to serve the rest of his life in prison for the exact same thing your husband did!"

She just sat there not even hearing me, only waiting for the answer to her question with no concern for me or my brother at all.

I looked at her with stone cold eyes and said: "If my son was your husband's, you would have never gotten to meet your grandson, and I would be dead."

I got up and left her sitting there speechless.

Mom always told us that if we ever needed a friend other than each other, she would be that friend. She proved to me that her husband, my abuser, had become her friend, and I was just an associate she happened to give birth to.

I prayed God would someday mend both our broken hearts.

Although I no longer considered my sister to be my best friend, I was able to forgive her because I found out our stepfather had abused her, too.

Even though there is no excuse for what she did, (REALITY) showed me that it is all part of the vicious cycle of abuse. I may not be guilty of the same thing as my sister, but I have found myself in negative situations and had surrendered to them.

Realizing that no matter where the affection comes from, we find ourselves surrendering to the fantasy of being wanted instead of "REALITY!"

Perhaps in "REALITY," this is what I have convinced myself to believe, because my sister still, to this day, denies having an affair with my ex-husband.

Nonetheless, this was a very hard situation to overcome.

Not wanting to become bitter, I allowed the situation to become my inspiration for this portion of the book, "Associate, Friend, or Enemy."

At the end of this chapter, if you still have a lot of friends, consider yourself to be blessed.

In others is where we place our friendship as well as our values.

Through experience I found this to be a very dangerous position to be in, because most people do not know the real meaning of a friend.

According to the Bible, a friend is someone that sticks closer than a brother/sister (Prov. 18:24: "A man that hath friends must shew himself friendly: and there is a friend that sticketh closer than a brother."), someone who loves and respects you at all times. (Prov. 17:17: "A friend loveth at all times, and a brother is born for adversity.") A friend will lay down their life for you. (John 15:13: "Greater love hath no man than this, that a man lay down his life for his friends.") Speaking of myself, I don't have too many friends that will do what the Bible says regarding a friend.

Puzzled by it all I looked up the word friend. While reading the definition of friend (Dictionary.com's version), two words stood out, giving me the "REALITY" check I needed to stop loosely calling everyone a friend. The words were "PERSONAL REGARD." This precisely described majority of the people I called a friend. They only had their personal regard in mind. Because most of the time I was the one giving. Not that I gave in order to receive, but it would have been nice if they would have occasionally done the same. Due to their own "PERSONAL REGARD" of getting more than giving they didn't reciprocate. When I stopped doing a lot of things, they stopped being the friends I believed I had. This has taught me an invaluable lesson: Never refer to someone as a friend before you really know them.

After learning the Biblical and literal versions of a friend, I now know that I have more dictionary friends than Biblical friends.

I have no problem with dictionary friends because I need them just as well as I need my few biblical friends.

Due to my past penchant for using the term "friend" so loosely, I asked God: "If people are nice to me, what do I refer to them as?"

After I spent many confused days and nights with this, I had an epiphany to use the word, "Associate" when referring to someone I do not truly know.

I looked up the word *associate* and it is "a person who shares actively in anything as business, enterprise, or undertaking; partner; colleague or a fellow worker."

I really had to try to make sense of this word "associate." Going back and re-reading the dictionary's version of a friend, I began to see how the definitions are slightly different friends have a personal regard for you; associates have a personal business regard with you.

Discovering that many people have attached themselves to me because they really care for me, however, "Reality" showed me: why wouldn't people attach themselves to a loving and giving person such as me? Especially once they realize they will certainly gain more than they give. Whether they gain financially, physically, emotionally or mentally, they still gain more than they give. Understand that God expects us to give; however, go to Him first when you begin to question your giving, and He will direct you. (Proverbs 3:6: "In all thy ways acknowledge Him and He shall direct thy paths.")

Make NO mistake about associates. They are wonderful to have, as long as you make sure you keep your eye on them.

I know who to consider my "friend" and who to consider an "associate" now.

My enemies can sometimes be hard to tell because they know how to disguise themselves well. After going through so much with both "friends" and "associates," I learned to spot my enemies quicker and with accuracy. Never taking my eyes off of my enemies because they are so clever, I learned they come in all shapes and colors, and tend to wear a beautiful smile.

This reminds me of the times when I would wake up for months to watch "Angel" and "Charmed" every morning at five o'clock. I would get so mad because I wanted to sleep.

Every morning my question to God was "WHY?" Seems like the more I asked why, the more I was awakened.

Therefore, I stopped asking why and just began to quiet my heart. I began to not only understand why, but to also see why it was important for me to watch these shows.

God was teaching me no matter what people look like, how well they speak, or where they come from, they can still be your enemy. In time, dealing with the invisible enemy, I discovered as long as I stood firm for what was right, they would leave, become one of my closest associates, or be a footstool. (Psalms 110:1 KJV: "The Lord said unto my Lord, Sit thou at my right hand, until I make thine enemies thy footstool.")

Now, ask yourself what type of friends do you have or are they really your enemies? For many, I am sure the dictionary wins by a landslide. Why does it have to be this way? The answer for me did not come easily because I based "friendship" according to the dictionary, not the Bible. Perhaps I convinced myself to believe that people just do not know how to be a friend. This may have been true to a certain degree. However, when I really began to put heart-felt emotions into the word *friendship*, I had to be realistic. Realistically speaking, I had to take an inventory of myself before I continued to allow people to enter into my life.

The "REALITY" of friendship is that many people do not know how to be a friend. Therefore, how can these people expect to have a friend? Speaking from my own perspective, I have tried to be a friend to any and every one that has come into my life. By doing so, I was left hurt and feeling betrayed by so many. I considered many of these people to be my friend.

Due to these so-called friends, I learned that everyone should not be recognized as a friend. I learned also that when you have too many friends, you set yourself up for heartache and disappointment as well.

It was during these heartbreaking experiences that I truly learned the difference between an associate, friend, and enemy.

I learned I could have as many associates as I liked, but when I got my associates mixed up with my friends, I couldn't see the enemy who was right in front of me. In most cases, I lost who could have been a true friend by trying to hold on to an associate that was, in "REALITY," my unsuspected enemy.

Associates have the tendency to make you believe that they are your friend simply because they are always there for you when you need them. I have learned that just because someone is there when you need them, doesn't qualify them to be considered a friend. Nine times out of ten, it simply makes them just plain ole nosy.

Think about it. How many times has Mister or Miss Associate been genuinely happy for you when you have good news to share?

Yes, they smile and cheer for you, but behind your back they make comments such as: "It's about time." "I can't believe it worked," and my all-time favorite, "If it wasn't for me, it would have never happened."

I think associates are really happy for you as long as they have something to gain or can take the credit for your accomplishments. If they can't get anything out of it, then they can't be bothered being with you or for you.

On the flip side, when there is bad news, they are right there beside you telling you how to or how not to handle the situation. How about when Mister or Miss Associate only come around when they have something good happen to or for them? They never come around when they have a problem, because they want you to believe their lives are perfect and problem-free. In "REALITY", their lives are a bigger mess than yours.

How about when you share an idea with Mister or Miss Associate, and they are so excited for you within your presence? You can best believe the minute you leave, they either take your idea or get busy telling other Associates how it's not going to work. News flash! A friend does not compete with you, they complete you. A friend never doubts what you are trying to accomplish. I am not saying that a friend cannot give you an opinion about whatever the situation may be. I'm saying that they should either support you or share their doubts with you, not with everyone else. I believe that God places people into our lives for different reasons, whether it's for a moment or for the long haul. By accepting REALITY, I have learned that whomever God places in my life for whatever length of time or for whatever reason, I'm going to care and share with them while I can.

I have learned to be realistic at all times regardless of my feelings towards people. When it's time for them to go, I let them go. By doing so, I have learned and accepted that you cannot keep someone that has no desire to be kept. You cannot hold on to someone who does not want to be held. Accepting (REALITY) has enriched me with the knowledge and wisdom to be wise when referring to someone as a friend.

Through my Biblical research, I have learned the value of all relationships, whether they are an Associate, Friend or an Enemy. You need each one of them to balance out your pathway to fulfill God's will for your life. You need **Associates** for assurance during the times when you have doubts within yourself. They become the driving force between success and failure. You need a **Friend** for endurance to be with you through all your ups and downs. They become the driving force of encouragement and understanding, which leads you to success, not failure. An **Enemy** is needed for insurance to keep you humble.

They become the driving force that will keep you centered and balanced so God can continue to grow and nurture you for His purpose. Assurance, endurance, and insurance all work for your benefit. Assurance builds your pride. Endurance builds your faith. By combining them together, you have the insurance needed to remain balanced and hopeful. Also, by combining the three together, you gain confidence, which grants you the ability to believe in yourself. (Philippians 4:13 KJV: "I can do all things through Christ which strengtheneth me.") With confidence, you do not need anyone to validate who you are. (Ephesians 2:10 KJV: "For we are his workmanship created in Christ Jesus unto good works, which God hath before ordained that we should walk in them.") You are equipped with the capability to walk through all trials and tribulations. You must stay balanced and not get pride and confidence mixed up.

How do you learn the difference between pride and confidence? Simply put: When you go into something with the consideration of others, that's confidence and success. When you go into something without the consideration of others, you are full of selfish pride, and failure is guaranteed'. (Pro. 16:18: "Pride goes before destruction, a haughty spirit before a fall.") Confidence is built on faith, which allows you to trust God no matter what the situation may be. (Pro. 3:5a: "Trust in the LORD with all thine heart; and lean not unto thine own understanding.") Pride is built on influence, which allows you to become a fool, so God can make you wise. (1 Cor. 3:18: "Let no man deceive himself. If any man among you seemeth to be wise in this world, let him become a fool, that he may be wise.")

Now that I have learned how to Biblically categorize the people in my life, I now know how to handle the trials, tribulations, and testimonies they may bring. If I get them confused, I sit quietly and wait on God, knowing that because He is with me, I will soon mount up with the wings of an eagle; soaring to my appointed destination so I can enjoy my destiny. (Is. 40:31: "But they that wait upon the LORD shall renew their strength; they shall mount up with wings as eagles; they shall run, and not be weary; and they shall walk, and not faint.")

Chapter 5
"Children Have Gone Wild"

"Lord, what the Hell is next? What did I do wrong? Unlike my mom, I was there for my boys! I never put anyone or anything before their well-being. I gave up my youth to make sure I was a good mother. Why does my baby boy have to go to prison?

I never bought them toy guns to play with, so how did my son end up with a gun to commit aggravated robbery?

"ATTENTION PARENTS! —Children have gone wild."

I didn't see the setup; now I do....

Setup #1:

Prayer is taken out of school

What a terrible mistake! If children did not attend church, at least during school, they got prayed for. The Bible clearly states that "where two or three are gathered together in my name, there am I in the midst of them" (Matt. 18:20 KJV). Why do you think God placed this Scripture in the Bible?

Let me explain: God knew there would be many among us who would not know how to pray nor care to pray. Because of His tender mercy, He placed and designed this Scripture to insure that those who knew how to pray would cover all those who could not or would not pray. God strategically placed His righteous ones in the schools to cover His little ones. I clearly remember when teachers would walk the halls, covering us with prayer and correction. They did not hesitate to say, "I am going to pray for your soul, child" or when you were not doing what was right, "God Don't Like Ugly." Can you imagine how great children would be if prayer and the name of God would have been kept in schools? No matter whether His name was used in prayer or in a simple sentence, His name kept children grounded.

Setup #2:

Corporal punishment taken out of school

What a bittersweet mistake. Yes, some people do not need to discipline children; however, some do need to be given the authority for discipline. School officials are filling in the gap for either working or absentee parents. They spend more time with our children than we do.

Children are in school for eight hours of learning. If they participate in any after-school activities, then two to three hours are added to the eight hours. Parents are not there to control their children's behavior, and we all know that children must have a consequence for misbehaving; who's there other than a school official? However, they are restricted from disciplining children due to state regulations.

What a mess we have created by supporting the removal of corporal punishment from school. Children are out of control and have absolutely no respect for adults! Now, the state has given children the right to disregard anyone who represents authority, rules or regulations; that's the law.

The Devil must be really proud because prisons and graves are full of children who could have possibly been saved by the presence of a disciplinarian.

I can remember when I was in school, the mere thought of having to go to the principal's office scared me straight.

Today children walk proudly to the principal's office, not scared of being punished. They quickly laugh in the face of a teacher when they even mention the principal's office.

The reason why children have no fear of authority is that the state has more control of children than parents.

Parents, I certainly pray that you see the error that has been made by not wanting anyone to discipline children, especially if the child belonged to you.

Flashing back in time, I still remember all the whipping's (a/k/a spankings) I got from people who were not my parents. If the neighbor saw me doing wrong, my parents expected me to be whipped. Then when I got home, I got another whipping for being a show-off. All those ole' sayings: "You don't believe fat meat is greasy," "It's time to pay the Piper," "You runnin' around thinkin' you grown. You ain't knee high to a duck," etc....These sayings were passed down for many generations; however, I am so glad we have better ways to explain how and why a child is going to get a spanking. They still make me laugh today.

I used to think my parents were crazy because whatever they grabbed first was the belt.

However, for the life of me, I never understood these three things when my parents wanted to whip me. They would tell me to go get my own switch; when I brought it to them, they would take all the leaves off, leaving the last two at the end of the switch, and then they had the nerve to say: "This is going to hurt me more than you."

First of all, did they really believe I was going to really pick a good one?

Secondly, leaving the two leaves at the end didn't make the whipping hurt any more.

Thirdly, how in the world was their whipping me going to hurt them more than me?

All I can do is laugh today still....

If children received the whippings I grew up getting, I truly believe they would behave a lot better, and crime would certainly be lower.

Of course, we know the times I was speaking of are so long ago—"REALITY"—that was then; this is now.

Children are fearless and have hardened their hearts. They commit crimes of hate, robbery, and murder without any remorse or concern for their victim, convinced rules and regulations don't apply to them. Thanks to the parents who insisted that corporal punishment be taken out of school, and also to the state for giving these parents what they wanted.

I am certain both the parents and the state see now what a terrible mistake they made. If not, the Devil has truly blinded them, and "REALITY" is nowhere to be found.

My "REALITY" check for both parents and the state is what my parents, neighbors, and school officials taught me: "Spare the rod, spoil the child" (see Pro.13:24 KJV).

As we can all clearly see, children are extremely spoiled, which makes them completely foolish. (Pro. 22:15 KJV: "Foolishness is bound in the heart of a child; but the rod of correction shall drive it far from him.")

No rod, no correction; no correction, no protection. Meaning if parents and the state are going to continue to stand in the way of the parents who want God to drive foolishness away from their child, crime is going to escalate beyond the state's control.

The state can build all the state jails and prisons they want. "REALITY" shows me it will do no good because God's Word is not being fulfilled.

Children have gone wild.

Seems to me if you refuse to discipline your children, you may need to ask yourself, "Do you love them?" If you love your children, you will discipline them with care. (Pro. 13:24 NLT: "He who spares the rod hates his son, but he who loves him is careful to discipline him.") Please do not misunderstand this Scripture.

In my opinion, God is simply saying that the same way He has to discipline us (Christians) for the things we do wrong, He expects us to discipline our children when they do things wrong. I am not saying that corporal punishment is needed at all times, but there are times when timeouts should be times in. Children quickly understand that all they have to do is be good for a short time, and they will be able to do what they want again.

I believe this is why we have so many repeat offenders within the judicial system now.

"REALITY" has proven prison will not rehabilitate inmates as long as they continue to have the luxuries of cable television and internet while in prison.

"REALITY" is proving in school that suspension does not change the majority of the children who know that good behavior for a while returns them back to their normal classroom in time.

"REALITY" check: Prison waits for many of the children who serve in school suspension regularly.

"REALITY" proves that serving a detention generally works only for those children who are not generally disruptive. However, for those who are constantly serving detention, "REALITY" check shows that the state jail waits for many of them.

The only time everyone should be serving is the time spent serving God!

Parents and state, when you have tried everything possible and nothing is working, corporal punishment (rod of correction) is the solution.

I know many parents will still disagree, but by the time God gets through allowing children to run wild, those who disagree will be the first ones to shout: "Get me my belt!" Taking corporal punishment out of school was Satan's second setup.

<u>Setup #3</u>

<u>"Uniforms" and "Education" are forced on children</u>

I am so glad that when I was in school, we were not forced to wear **"uniforms."** How in the world could this be best for children? This benefits whom? The only ones to benefit from forcing uniforms as a requirement are the companies who make them. Parents and children certainly do not benefit in any way. Parents don't benefit because they still have to buy the uniforms that are not as durable as denim jeans. The cotton material used shrinks faster because most companies do not use pre-shrunk cotton material when making the clothing.

Children don't benefit because they lose their individuality. They are forced to look like each other.

This has to be confusing for the children in school. Why do I say this? "REALITY" is proving boys look like girls and girls look like boys. This may not always be the case, but it sure makes it easier for Satan to manipulate the minds of children. This gives Satan the perfect opportunity to place in the minds of boys who have feminine ways that they can be a girl and girls who have masculine ways that they can be a boy. Since everyone looks the same, it's okay to act the same for those boys and girls who have the tendency to act more like the opposite sex.

Think about it: boys don't wear skirts, so it would be harder to let their tendencies be seen, and girls don't wear shirts that are clearly designed for boys.

Having every child dressed the same creates a mess of acceptable confusion within the schools.

Don't get me wrong; I'm not saying that if a child is attracted to the same sex, the confusion wouldn't happen if uniforms were not being enforced.

I am simple saying it sure makes the unnatural behavior easier to overlook and accept. We are living in the last days and perilous times.

"REALITY" is written!!!! (2 Tim. 3:1–3 KJV: (1) "This know also, that in the last days perilous times shall come. (2) For men shall be lovers of their own selves, covetous, boasters, proud, blasphemers, disobedient to parents, unthankful, unholy, (3) Without natural affection, trucebreakers, false accusers, incontinent, fierce, despisers of those that are good, ...")

"Education"

Did I say **"education?"**

Yes, I did.

It is a shame that Satan has been able to use education to manipulate the world.

Please do not misunderstand me. Education is wonderful, but if it takes a degree for someone to be considered educated, then I guess I am a dummy. I do not have a degree, and I was not the best writer in school, but here I am writing a book. I have faith, which gives me the will power to write from experience and from my hunger to acquire knowledge from the lessons I've learned living everyday life.

Looking up education on dictionary.com I found that school had nothing to do with its definition of education.

If children, with the exception of those who may be mentally challenged, have the ability to learn basic fundamentals, such as eating or going to the bathroom, then they have the capability to acquire knowledge.

Generation to generation has proven that genetics impact the development of a child. If a child comes from a family of educated doctors, then more than likely the child will become a doctor. Not because of a school, but because he was born into a family of educated doctors. "REALITY" tells me that since most of his family members were probably educated doctors, he knew what a stethoscope was without any schooling, more likely than not.

"REALITY" **check**: It was the parents' experience at that point in time educating the child, not a school teacher.

Please take no offense—the teacher is important during a child's developmental stages, because they help enhance what the parents may have already started teaching their child. Both parents and teachers play a significant role in helping a child gain the ability to intellectually advance in maturity.

Because of the state government's greed (inflated school taxes), parents are forced to send their children to school to pay for an education (higher than High School) that has the possibility in some cases to be taught for free.

I remember watching "Gun-smoke" as a child, thinking, "How did Doc (the town's doctor) become a doctor? He never went to school anytime during the show, but he was the town's doctor. Since it was not clear how Doc became a doctor I will assume he must have learned everything from his parents or from the experience of trial and error.

"REALITY": I never saw him sitting in a classroom paying to be taught. (Please take no offense to this analogy because Doc may have paid for his education; it was never stated nor implied during any of the shows I watched.)

True "REALITY": Today most people believe that children must have some form of higher education other than a high school diploma in order to live comfortably. However, God is the true giver of everything, and if children are taught to love Him by someone who loves Him. "ALL" things work together according to His purpose (Ro. 8:28 KJV: "And we know that all things work together for good to them that love God, to them who are called according to his purpose"), educated or not. Loving God first in my opinion will put you on the right path needed for all things to work according to His purpose. I also believe education certifies one to use a title/s and experience qualifies one to educate others using personal experience/s.

Setup # 4

Evolution of Technology

The **evolution of technology** is by far the craftiest setup Satan is using.

Technology allows Satan to enter into homes in many ways. Here are the craftiest technological resources Satan has used according to what I believe. They are **television**, **cellphones,** and **computers**.

How so?

Glad you asked.

Most shows produced today for television are very deceiving. A majority of the shows being aired promote unnatural affection, violence, sex, and drugs.

Cartoons are no longer gender-specific—most of the characters look and sound alike.

I was watching cartoons with my granddaughter, and was totally confused. I couldn't tell if the character was a boy or a girl.

I asked my granddaughter if she knew who was the boy or girl, and she said, "Gigi, I think the one with the blue shirt on is the boy, and the girl is the one with the red shirt on."

I was immediately alarmed by her response because she said "I think," trying to help me figure out their genders.

Still not satisfied, I asked her "Why do you say the boy is the one with the blue shirt on and the girl has the red shirt on?"

She looked at me like I was asking her a dumb question before she answered. She said, "Because boys wear blue and girls wear red."

This bothered me even more, so I said, "You wear blue, too."

Before I could ask her anymore questions, she said, "I'm sleepy."

I knew this was the end of my questions.

It saddens me to know that children can "NO" longer tell if it's a boy or girl playing the role of a character. The hairstyles are the same for both characters, they are dressed the same, and they sound the same.

Sitcoms used to promote family unity; not any more. Most sitcoms are more about being funny versus family. I am not saying that there are not any great family sitcoms; I'm saying they may start out good, but it's a bunch of nothing towards the end of the series.

Why do I say this?

Because I can remember watching sitcoms as a child, and I don't remember any of the teenagers having a child without a husband; I don't remember seeing the parents lying in bed together having sex; I don't remember seeing men sleeping with men or women sleeping with women; and I definitely don't remember hearing profanity being used during the show.

I can even speak about television videos.

As a child, videos were child-friendly. Meaning if I was watching a video regarding a song I still did not know the true meaning of the song after watching the video.

A prime example of a child-friendly video I remember watching as a child: the song was "Atomic Dog" song by George Clinton. As a child I thought it was a song about a dog chasing a cat. I had no idea that the song was not about a real dog chasing a cat. The video just showed women looking like cats dancing, and a man was playing video games. This as a child made me believe the people in the video were just having fun playing games and dancing to the music. It wasn't until much later in life that I found out that the song was about a man chasing a woman.

Most songs and videos today are not child-friendly; the songs and videos clearly explain what the song is about.

Example: if the song is about a girl kissing a girl, then the video shows nothing but girls sexually dancing with other girls and kissing each other.

If the song is about ballin' (a street term that describes the way a person makes a lot of money whether it is legally or illegally obtained) as a child, my imagination would have me thinking the video would be about a game being played with a ball. However, my imagination would be shattered because the videos regarding ballin', clearly gives a definition of ballin'.

In such videos, children today see men with their pants hanging down selling drugs on the corners, with cars painted to perfection with huge shiny rims on the tires that are worth more than the car. God forbid, if children do not notice the blinged-out (today's terminology for real/fake diamonds) teeth in the mouth of the star of the video, which clearly matches his huge shiny rims. They must not be able to see. To complete the star-studded appearance, they have tattoos covering most of their body, smiling and grinning hard as though they just won video of the year.

I tell you, the rims and teeth are so shiny if you see them in the sun, you will for sure suffer temporary blindness because of all the bling-bling. The video makes the driver look as though he or she is having so much fun because they are holding a wad of money in their hands while a wad of money is falling out of their pockets.

The girls in the videos are barely dressed, because their shorts are in their behind, and breasts are stuffed into a too-little shirt. Heels are high enough to snatch an airplane out of the sky, and they're dancing like they are ready to be gang-raped. Makeup is so heavy a clown's makeup is applied to light to be considered a clown. She is happy to be dancing, riding, or sleeping with the guy with the big shiny-rimmed car and teeth that match.

However, nowhere in the video do you see "REALITY." Children, this is not a glamorous life. Only **three things** come from this lifestyle: a **felony record, jail or imprisonment, or death;** nothing else.

"REALITY" **check**: "Men learn the value of an honest dollar, and girls learn that you are worth more than a dollar!"

Here's how **"cellphones"** fit within Satan's control of children.

It is almost a necessity for a child to have a cellphone, because crime has gotten so far out of hand. Due to the escalation of crime, it is a must that all responsible children have a cellphone. However, parents, there are a few things you should understand before and after you make your purchase.

Understand that children having cellphones gives Satan a direct line of hidden communication. This leaves you with no way of knowing who they are talking to or what about. At least with land lines, parents may not have known what the conversation was about, but they certainly would know who the conversation was with, because all a parent had to do was pick up another phone in the house and they would be able to hear the entire conversation or look at the caller ID.

Once again, "That was then; this is now!" Children are taking advantage of parents' purchase of a cellphone for them. They use their cellphone for everything except for their safety, leaving Satan in most cases in complete control.

So parents, please carefully monitor your children's phone activity. Satan manipulates parents into believing if they check the call logs or text messages, they are invading their child's privacy, but with the way the world is today, privacy is not up for negotiation, parents! Privacy invasion is saving many lives of children, especially where verbal communication in a lot of households is NO longer, which is Satan's direct line to the mindset of children.

How so?

If there is no verbal communication between children and parents at home, Satan can use whoever and whatever is needed to gain complete control over children. This is why it is so important to talk to your children instead of sending a text message to them. It is imperative that children know that they have a sounding board at home.

Parents know that there is no conversation outside of your home more important than the conversation between you and your children inside your home, because the conversation you have with your children at home may be used to encourage the children who do not have a good conversation at home nor a healthy home life.

Besides, parents, children feel a sense of pride when they can share something they have been taught at home with someone else.

Another way Satan is able to use the cell-phones is by picture mail.

Did I say that? Yes I did, and here's how.

Picture mail was meant to be something good—a way of sharing a smile or precious memories, but now Satan has perverted it into filth. Children as well as some parents of children are not sending only friendly pictures. They are now sending grimy, sexual pictures.

Speaking from experience, I had been asked by a male acquaintance to send a picture of myself, and when I sent the picture, I was asked if I minded showing a little skin? Of course, I knew what he was asking, but I was not going to exploit nor degrade my character for a man that had nothing on his mind other than sex. Trying to give him the benefit of the doubt, I sent him a picture of my foot, and he got mad and said to me, "If you want to play games, go find someone else." I said to him, "If you want a sexy picture showing skin, go buy a Playboy magazine." Needless to say, our texting one another ended as well as our phone calls.

I also had another horrible experience because of the cellphone. I was in New York City when I left my cellphone in a taxi cab. I was completely lost because I did not know any phone number other than my son's number, which served no purpose because he was in Texas. Long story short, I was blessed to get back to the hotel without an incident, and it was the eye opener I needed to stop Satan from making a fool out of me. I started memorizing phone numbers again as well as directions.

Parents, there is a reason why cellphones are no longer called cellphones; they are now called "Smartphones," and indeed they are smarter than a fifth grader. Satan's smartphone is a lure that is going to have ninety percent of the world needing to be hooked on phonics, stuck on stupid or dead from texting while driving.

Although smartphones are somewhat of a necessity for safety purposes, nonetheless parents, do all that you can to encourage your children to continue to use correct grammar, and remember important phone numbers and directions. These three things can be the difference between life and death.

Satan has to be sitting back laughing, knowing that the plans he made are working fully.

Here are three key reasons as to why Satan's set-ups are working and proving without a doubt why "Children Have Gone Wild":

Reason #1

Love is not being taught! Parents have so much going on that they do not realize they are now teaching foolishness, disobedience, hate, greed, and envy because of the "Keep up with the Joneses" mentality. (Tit. 3:3 KJV: "For we ourselves also were sometimes foolish, disobedient, deceived, serving divers lusts and pleasures, living in malice and envy, hateful, and hating one another."). The love of material things is what children are learning, not love for one another. Many parents are teaching this unintentionally, because most parents want their children to have the things they did not have when they were their child's age. I am not saying parents should not give their children most of the things they want. What I am saying is that if giving your children what they want causes you to spend more time away from home than at home, you are placing your children in a position for Satan to maneuver. Satan is very crafty when it comes to manipulating you into his method of madness.

Satan gets us caught up with loving things more than we love people. Parents, we must teach our children to love others first and then things. Love should be taught from the beginning (1 Jn. 3:11 KJV: "For this is the message that ye heard from the beginning, that we should love one another.")

Parents, God allowed this Scripture to be strategically placed in the Bible as the foundation for all to live successfully in this world. How can you live in this world successfully without love?

It is impossible!

Why do you think so many children start out innocent, but end up being murderers, drug addicts, prostitutes, or career criminals? They fall in love with their own selfish passions. Although some parents may believe they thought it was love, my question is what kind of love is being or has been taught? Most parents have and are teaching selfish love instead of self-love. This is the common mistake I believe parents have made unintentionally. Parents try very hard to make sure that their children love themselves, but sometimes so much emphasis is put on self-love that children get confused, turning self-love into selfish love. The reason for this is because parents start out simply trying to meet their children's wants instead of their needs. For instance, your children come home and say, "I saw a girl or boy at school with a shirt that I like; can you buy me one?" Sure, you can agree to purchase your child that shirt, but find out the reason for that shirt. Is it something that your child really needs or is it just something they want? Am I saying you should not get some of your children's wants? No, I am saying find out why your child wants that shirt. Is it because they just want something that someone else has? Are they trying to compete with that child, or do they simply want the shirt out of admiration? You might be surprised or get surprised by their answer.

Reason #2

"Parents are gone wild!" Men are on vacation and women are looking for a vacation. Who's there for the children? I'll tell you, Satan's society and the streets. Parents, if you do not take the time to raise your children, Satan's society and the streets will gladly do it for you. It is sad to see the way children are being neglected in order for parents to pursue their happiness. Whether the parent(s) pursuit of happiness is in their career, drugs, alcohol, a man, a woman, or whatever they are after, it should be put on hold until they have laid the foundation of love. This is why we have so many self-absorbed children in the world today; they have no one teaching them the foundation of love for "thy neighbor" (others). This is the royal law of God: "Love Thy Neighbor" (James 2:8 KJV: "If ye fulfil the royal law according to the scripture, Thou shalt love thy neighbour as thyself, ye do well.") If children have not been taught to obey this law, then how can they obey the laws of society? It can't be done; just look at the crime rate today amongst the children.

Parents, when you seek after money more than you teach love, you will never have enough and will be of no help to anyone. (1 Jn. 3:17 NLT: "But if anyone has enough money to live well and sees a brother or sister in need and refuses to help—how can God's love be in that person?")

God knew that this was going to happen because He knew that parents or other adults would become so full of greed for the things of this world, they would not only neglect each other, but their children, too!

Parents, I can assure you that God is not pleased with the neglecting of children; this is why: He is allowing so much to happen right before your very eyes. For example: Parents are afraid to be the parents, and adults are too afraid to speak up for the parents. Parents and adults, if you want God to stop this terror amongst children, go back to the basics. Teach children to abide in faith, hope, and charity (which means the benevolent goodwill toward, or love of, humanity) for one another. God says the greatest of these three is charity (1 Co. 13:13: "And now abideth faith, hope, charity, these three; but the greatest of these is charity.") Parents, I urge you to stop what you are doing and pay attention to your children. Give them that kiss of love, that hug of strength, or that caress of caring; whatever your children need, take the time out to give it to them.

Reason #3

Success, success, success! This is all children hear in a majority of homes today. They are told repeatedly that education is the key to success. Again, education is wonderful if children are pursuing a career that requires furtherance in education; then continually encourage children to obtain their educational goals. However, parents have gone overboard with the term *success*! Now because of parents' lust for success, no matter what they need to do, it will be done in order to accomplish their dream of success, even if it's through their children.

Parents, your job is not to force success on your child/children, but to teach your children the desire to be successful; do not teach them that at all cost, they must become a success. Too many emphases have been put on success and less on love by parents and society. Parent(s), I understand you want your children to be successful; however, the "REALITY" is all children are not meant to be successful. But I do know that all are to be loved. Instead of forcing children to become successful, why not teach them to love? It is so sad that our children desire material things more than being loving. Love is not something that should be desired; it is a commandment (Jn. 15:12 KJV: "This is my commandment, That ye love one another, as I have loved you."). Parents, love is the greatest thing that children should be taught. Teaching children about love will bring charity amongst children instead of conflict.

Charity is the outcome of love, and the doorway to success, parents!

Can children be successful without love?

Absolutely not!

Why?

In order to become a success you have to at some point make your children love the idea of success. If you cannot get them to love success, then you can certainly get them to love the material things success brings. But in doing so always teach your children that it is not material things that make them a success it is their love for the material things that forces them to become a success. However, they must still treat all with dignity, and respect, and always be willing to help someone along the way freely. Love is a must! Without love, how can they convince others to help and share with them? This is where charity comes in; if you have not taught your children love, then do not expect others to teach them the kind of love you as a parent want your child to know. If you want your child to have Godly love then you must teach it. If not rest assured Satan's workers will teach them to love according to the world (same sex relationships, porn, fornication, drugs, etc.). Hello parents! Are you beginning to get the message? Well, perhaps some of you are not. The message is: if you have not taught your children love, then they have missed the key element in success, which is charity. Because of charity, you teach them faith to believe and give them the hope needed to achieve their dreams. Parents love and charity work go hand-in-hand with each other, but the greater of these two in my opinion is love. Without love, children will feel nothing for anyone leaving them compassionless for others, even if they have success along with the material things of this world; they will still not be happy, and neither will you!

Parents, allow your children to become what they want instead of what you want them to become. Stop trying to develop your children into you or your dreams. Is it okay to dream big for your children? But remember, children do start out developing into what you (parents) desire them to be, but also they eventually develop their own desires. Parents, I am not talking about something I have not been through myself with my own children.

Let me give you my story, the night I had to accept my "REALITY" of "A Mother's Cry." (My definition of this cry is when a mother has done all she can do to save her child from going in the wrong direction, but her child is determined to do it the wrong way. It is at this point all she can do is release her child and allow life to take its course. Knowing her child may end up facing some form of pain and she can do nothing but cry when prayer seems not to be enough or not working).

All I could do was cry out, "God help me! My son is determined to go in the wrong direction." The pain ripped to the very depths of my inner soul. The pain was so severe, I could hardly breathe; with every breath I took, it felt like my heart stopped between each beat. "Oh, God" was all I could manage to get out when the pain erupted from within me. Liquid was all that managed to come out of my mouth as I struggled to breathe. The pain within me was relentless as it continued with a vengeance raging through my body. With each twinge of aching pain, there came out of me a mother's worst wail—I call "A Mother's Cry"— moaning God to have mercy on me because my son had just been sentenced to ten years in prison. For those of you reading who are mothers, this is a cry you never want to experience. Your child is either dead, out of control headed for death, or on their way to prison. Perhaps you have yet to experience this pain, and I pray that you never have to in order to understand it. However, if you are a mother who has had to release your children to the world against your better judgment, then this is pain you can understand. I have seen many mothers experience this pain, but I never thought nor imagined how immense the pain could be until it happened to me. It was like a ball of fire in the form of a liquid, caught between my throat and stomach, suffocating my heart. I felt like I was going to have a heart attack. I knew the only way to stop the pain was to release the liquid, but I was afraid to let it come up. Therefore, I tried to force myself not to release the ball of liquid fire within, and I strained and struggled to hold back the eruption of pain that had transformed itself into liquid fire with all my might, but to no avail; this liquid erupted like a volcano releasing hot lava. I barely made it to the bathroom. After cleaning myself up, I was left drained of emotions; I could barely walk; I was numb inside; all I managed to mumble was, "God, please help me." As I laid my head onto my fluffy pillow, I hoped my river of tears would take me to a more peaceful place. I tried to stop the tears, but the emotional currents inside me were much too strong; so I had to let the tears flow. Tears of fear, helplessness, and anger flowed relentlessly from my eyes. Not able to take anymore, I began to talk to God saying, "I know I am supposed to trust you at all times, but I'm not understanding why. I have been the best mother, never missing a school party, always on the sideline of every game, coaching and cheering, hoping and praying constantly, but to no avail. Somewhere, somehow, I feel like I failed in spite of all my efforts." Before I could say anything else, the Holy Spirit came over me, gently soothing me, and I heard these words, "You have laid a solid foundation of love; now allow Me to build on it." Due to my not wanting to let go and let God, my son began to disrespect me; he began to not value my opinion, leaving me feeling unappreciated.

Even though I said with my mouth I trusted God, "REALITY" showed me that I really didn't trust God completely. I was still trying to get respect from my son by giving an opinion or seeking validation, hoping he would start to appreciate me.

It wasn't until after many days and nights of disrespect, I finally realized that the only way my son was going to give me the respect I rightfully deserved was when I truly trusted God and released my son to experience life. I began to trust

God with my mind, body, and soul, and once I began to completely trust God, I was able to peacefully rest. I found comfort in this Scripture: "Thou wilt keep him in perfect peace, whose mind is stayed on thee: because he trusteth in thee. 4Trust ye in the LORD forever: for in the LORD JEHOVAH is everlasting strength" (Is. 26:3-4: KJV).

Mothers, I know it is hard to let go of our child/children once they reach a certain age because we know their eyes still have not been open long enough to understand the ways of the world. But, the "REALITY" of it all is if you do not trust God, you will find yourself in a world of turmoil, delaying God from answering your prayers for your child/children. How could God answer my prayer/s as long as I remained in the way, trying to fix a situation that was too big for me to handle. While looking at my son, I realized that I had to close my heart to self and let him go; in order for God to grow him into the man he was put here on earth to be. When you accept "REALITY," regardless of how hard it is, you will be left with no choice other than to release your child/children into the world of adulthood. When you have instilled your child/children with good moral values, do not worry; they may stray, but trust me when I tell you that God will handle the situation perfectly (Pro. 22:6 KJV: "Train up a child in the way he should go: and when he is old, he will not depart from it.").In reality, God will allow your child/children to go through things in order to reveal Himself to you or through you. God only reveals Himself in His desired timing, which is for His purpose.

Once you accept God's timing, you will then be able to give Him all the glory. It is at this time that God will get your attention or get the attention of your child/children(s), drawing all focus onto Him by opening all ears to hear and hearts to receive His voice. During this time, you will discover what your child/children are going to go through, but as long as you realize that it is your job to pray and trust God and not try to rush Him, your child/children will survive and overcome their storms. (1 John 4:4: KJV: "Ye are of God, little children, and have overcome them: because greater is he that is in you, than he that is in the world.").

"REALITY": Parents, do not be in denial when it comes to who your child/children become or what they do. The longer you remain in denial, God can't fix them. They usually end up dead, imprisoned, or living a non-productive life because of denial. Parents—especially mothers—let go; God has it under control!

Chapter 6
Forbidden Love

T rying to digest the "REALITIES", engulfing me: being sexually molested, my mother asking me if my son was her husband's son, the acceptance of my prince still being a frog who would rather kiss other women including my sister instead of me, and my baby boy going to prison; left me feeling like he leaped into water too deep for me to save him. Hopeless and helpless, but most of all heartbroken these harsh "Realities" caused me to become withdrawn and depressed. I began to look for ways to escape just so I would not have to deal with what I couldn't handle. I thought about going to the club, but since I really didn't want to be bothered with the party crowd, that was out. I didn't want to go to the church because I was angry at God for not helping me, hearing me, or saving me from this bottomless pit of pain. I knew "I" needed to get it together because my mind was moving faster than my body, heart aching and nerves were fraying. I didn't want to have a nervous breakdown which was sure to happen if "I" didn't do something to feel somewhat normal again. I tried praying, but God was not answering me fast enough, leaving me angry and determined not to have a nervous breakdown, lose my mind or spend another night in the house staring at the walls feeling as though I was about to lose control. Every night after I put my boys to bed I went into my nightly routine of crying and rocking back and forth, asking over and over again, "Why me, Lord?" I had to get out of this pit of doom somehow, someway, so I called the only person I knew and trusted, Shay.

Shay, "I am so bored!" I have to get out of this house! It's killing me to keep sitting here trying to cope with all that has happened in the last few months. I need to do something, but what is there to do?" I asked my friend Shay, who was just breathing into the phone not saying anything.

Finally, she said, "Let's go to Chili's to eat and have a drink."

I was so bored, I quickly agreed. "I'll meet you there at eight-thirty tonight."

She said, "Okay, see you in a few."

"Okay, girl," I said. Before I could get "Bye" out, she had already hung up on me.

I chuckled as I headed to get dressed, smiling the entire time because I was finally getting out of the house to have a great time and hopefully, meet a nice guy.

I got to Chili's before Shay. I decided to go to the bar and order a drink (Coke) while I waited for Shay.

"Hey, sexy lady, what can I get you to drink?" The bartender asked all cheerily.

"I'll have a coke."

He looked at me as if he was shocked. "A coke only?" he asked.

"Yes, I don't drink," I said with a lick of my lips, dragging my tongue slowly back into my mouth with a hint of seduction, which clearly indicated I was single and ready for conversation..

He was a cutie.

I made sure it was not a secret about my attraction to him. But I guess he was not interested; he winked and said, "You better be careful with your sexiness; you never know who's watching," as he turned to go and wait on other customers.

"You must not be a drinker," a woman sitting not far from me said.

"No, I'm not," I said, trying to make sure she knew our conversation was over before it got started.

She was sitting there looking like a dude. I was hoping and praying she didn't think I was interested in her.

I could see how she may have gotten the wrong impression about me because I wore my haircut extremely short.

As I looked at the chick dude sitting one chair over from me, all I could do was think about what my sons said to me, "Mom, you look like a cute boy."

I laughed at them and said, "Well, I'm not a boy. I'm all woman," while tracing a silhouette of my curvy figure.

"Okay, when them She'em's (which they called women who were trying to be men) start trying to talk to you, don't say we didn't warn you."

"I hope a She'em doesn't make that mistake, because she will see a side of me that ain't nice."

"Man, you hear your Mama trying to sound gangster!" my younger son (who always has something to say) said to his older brother, laughing and throwing up make-believe gang signs.

"Whatever; like I said, a She'em better not make that mistake!"

"Man, Lil Bro, I hope a She'em doesn't try, because we know she can go ghetto gangster."

We all laughed....

Stirring me from my reminiscing was the chick dude (aka She'em), who was now sitting on the stool right next to me.

Oh, H*, let me get my gangsta on! I knew I was going to need it by the way she was leaning on the bar like she was a real man seriously ready to flirt.

"You mind if I sit here," she asked.

"Nope, it's not my seat," I said with an attitude, looking in the opposite direction.

"What brings a sexy woman like you out tonight?" she asked.

Oh yeah; she's going there. I feel myself getting ready to explode on her, but before I could, Shay walked up.

"What's up, Sharon?"

"Not a d* thing," I said, lookin' at the She'em sittin' there staring Shay down.

"D*, what's wrong with you?" Shay asked, not paying any attention to the She'em.

She knew something had to be wrong with me if I was cussing. I very seldom used cuss words, but when I did, everyone knew I had to be mad or have an attitude about something.

"Nothing; let's go get us a table before I lose it in here." I was up and walking out of the bar before Shay could blink.

"Alright already," Shay said, as she turned to catch up with me.

Once seated, I told Shay what was going on, and she laughed at me until tears were coming out of her eyes.

"We tried to tell you that you made a cute She'em."

I gave Shay a go-to–H* look, and we both laughed so hard.

"Well I guess she must think I'm your wo-"Man," I said.

"When I walked up, the She'em was sitting there like a mannequin; that's why I didn't pay her any attention," Shay said, still laughing uncontrollably.

All I can say is, these gay people are out of control. I have nothing against gays, but they really need to stop the madness.

"Sharon, what are you talking about? Now, girl, you act like you hate gay people."

"That's not it at all; besides if it were true, then I would have to hate our best friend Nikki, and you know I love her to death."

"Uh oh, watch it now; are you —?"

Before Shay could finish her question, I cut her off. "Don't play with me; you know how much I love men. All I'm saying is if they are going to be gay, let them stop trying to talk to every woman that they think is cute. Nikki doesn't do that with women.

"Shay, don't keep sitting over there giving me crazy looks as though you are clueless. If God wanted women to be with women, He wouldn't have created men."

"Well, Miss Sharon, how do you plan on living in this world? We are surrounded by gay people."

"As I said, I don't agree with their choice of living, but as a believer of Christ, all I can do is tell them what the Bible says and move on. I don't have to watch them kiss and hug on each other like its normal. That's the only way I can deal with Nikki. She knows how I feel about her choice; that's why, when she comes to visit and has a chick with her, you never know if it's her friend or her wo-"Man." She is respectful of others regardless of her choice."

"I hear you," Shay said. "Well girl, let's not worry about that because they are in God's hands."

"You're right, Shay, but that kind of love just is not natural and is forbidden by God. H*, they wouldn't exist if God didn't create a man and woman. How can two men or two women have kids? The Bible says for us to be fruitful and multiply."

"That's a good question. I guess when we see Nikki, we can ask her how she would have been born if a man didn't get her mother pregnant which produced her."

"Shay girl, you know Nikki's going to come up with some scientific reasoning to right her lifestyle. Especially since she truly has convinced herself to believe that although she was born a woman, God created her to be a man."

Sharon, I know you've got to be kidding. Nikki ain't ever said that s* in front of me!" Shay said, while looking at She'em.

"Now you see where I'm coming from with that craziness. Again, it ain't natural and besides, 'if it don't make book sense or common sense, it's nonsense,'" I said, as we walked past the She'em on our way out the door.

That was the end of our conversation about Nikki and her absurd lifestyle and belief.

This experience was my motivation for this chapter, "Forbidden Love." During this time I was at the lowest point in my life and began seeking a way to escape my "REALITY" rather than wait on God to renew my strength. I placed myself in a situation that could have easily led me further astray from God. I thank God that His mercy and grace kept me from falling. (Ephesians 2:8 KJV: "For by grace are ye saved through faith; and that not of youselves: it is the gift of God.")

To have love for others is truly the greatest thing God has given us the ability to do. Loving others should be the one thing that we show and express daily towards one another. However, when this love is taken to the level in which men begin to love men and women begin to love women in the same way that God designed and designated for a man and a woman, this is unacceptable. It is what I call "forbidden love." God is not pleased with those who choose to love someone of the same sex intimately. This love is forbidden. It will make you become delusional in the mind, leaving you to believe that you are doing something acceptable because God created you this way, so it's not your fault that you are how you are. This is a lie! Everything that God made is good and perfect. If God created you to be a male in your mother's womb, then you are a man, not a woman; If God created you to be female in your mother's womb, then you a woman, not a man. (Genesis 1:27 KJV: "So God **created** man in **his** own **image**, in the **image** of God **created** he him; male and female **created** he them.") No matter how you try to recreate yourself into your own image, you cannot, because God created you in His image, and because He is perfect (Matthew 5:48 KJV: "Be ye perfect, even as your Father which is in heaven is perfect."), He does not need you to try and change what He created perfectly.

135

ATTENTION ALL HOMOSEXUALS AND LESBIANS!

This is a trick of the devil to make you believe that it is okay for you to love someone of the same sex in the same way God demanded, designed, and designated for a man and woman to enjoy. For those of you who are in this type of relationship it may be hard to accept that God is not pleased; He destroyed an entire city because of the unnatural affection within the city. (Jude 7 KJV: "Even as Sodom and Gomorrha, and the cities about them in like manner, giving themselves over to fornication, and going after strange flesh, are set forth for an example, suffering the vengeance of eternal fire.") I know no one sin is greater than another, but God destroyed a whole city because of their unnatural affection.

For years, we have been told and taught that God loves everybody no matter what. God does love us all, but when you do something that is not of Him, He still can love you, but God does not accept you as His own. If you are one that is in this position, know that God is not pleased with your choice, and

He will disown you. If you don't believe me, read it for yourself: 26For this cause God gave them up unto vile affections: for even their women did change the natural use into that which is against nature: 27And likewise also the men, leaving the natural use of the woman, burned in their lust one toward another; men with men working that which is unseemly, and receiving in themselves that recompence of their error which was meet. 28And even as they did not like to retain God in their knowledge, God gave them over to a reprobate mind, to do those things which are not convenient; 29Being filled with all unrighteousness, fornication, wickedness, covetousness, maliciousness; full of envy, murder, debate, deceit, malignity; whisperers, 30Backbiters, haters of God, despiteful, proud, boasters, inventors of evil things, disobedient to parents, 31Without understanding, covenant breakers, without natural affection, implacable, unmerciful: 32Who knowing the judgment of God, that they which commit such things are worthy of death, not only do the same, but have pleasure in them that do them. (Ro: 1:26-32 KJV) These verses clearly explain to you what God will do to those who have unnatural love for others. I am not condemning those who live this way, God is. Please, those of you who feel this type of behavior is of God open your eyes and read the Scriptures so you will know that this is unacceptable to God. I know that there are many "believers" in this type of unnatural love; it is truly forbidden by God; no matter how you try to make it make sense, it doesn't. I challenge all the preachers, teachers, bishops, clergymen, elders, apostles, pastors, priests, or anyone else who represents Christ to start speaking the truth about this unnatural, forbidden love, and watch and see how God will come in and heal the land.

I remember there was a time when those who practiced living this way would be ashamed to show their affectionate love in public. But because Christians have become so focused on the blessings of God and not the curses, Satan is manipulating Christians until they have forgotten to pray against these curses. The "REALITY" is that this unnatural love is absolutely and totally out of control. If you don't believe that God is upset, you better think again. Not only is God upset about the unnatural love, he is not pleased with married people going outside of their marriage for intimacy or whatever it is they are looking for outside of their marriage. This is adultery, and it is a sin worthy of death, too. (Lev. 20:10 KJV: "And the man that committeth adultery with another man's wife, even he that committeth adultery with his neighbour's wife, the adulterer and the adulteress shall surely be put to death.") When you marry someone, you are supposed to love that person no matter what. I know it gets hard sometimes to deal with the one you have married, but you have committed yourself to this person, so therefore, you have to find a way to overcome the hard times. I truly believe that when you marry someone, you should have the same goals for the future, in the same income bracket, with the same family values and morals. If you marry before you take these things into consideration, you will be taking a chance on stepping out of the marriage, seeking that which is missing.

However, if you pray and ask God to forgive you for not waiting on Him, he will turn your marriage into all you expect and more or allow you to have peace while going through a divorce. I know a lot of Christians do not believe in divorce, but it happens. Most people get married before they have a personal relationship with Christ and are hurt so badly by the person "they" chose to marry in many cases forces them to turn to God to be relieved by Him before they believed in Him. "REALITY" I am one who can speak from experience regarding marrying before having a relationship with Christ this is why I am a divorcee. Now that I have a personal relationship with Christ I will not rush into marriage again. I will wait on God to be chosen by a man who loves Christ and has a relationship with Him. It is my belief that God does not want His children to stay in a marriage that he did not put together. Therefore, if you are in a struggle with the one you have married pray and ask God for guidance and if you are to divorce God will give you peace while you are going through. On the other hand, if you know God has joined you with the one you are going to marry or have married let "NO" man separate you. (Matt. 19:5-6 KJV: 5 And said, for this cause shall a man leave father and mother, and shall cleave to his wife: and they twain shall be one flesh? 6 Wherefore they are no more twain, but one flesh. What therefore God hath joined together, let not man put asunder.)

Hold on, I'm not through yet! For all those who love to have premarital sex, God isn't pleased with you either. This is unnatural love because you fall in love with the sex before you get to know the person. This is also why we have so many divorces in the world today. Sex before marriage is a good feeling, but it isn't right. I am guilty of this myself; this is why I can tell you that this is unnatural love, because I know what it is to love the physical more than you do the person.

However, "REALITY" has taught me that if the physical is all you have, then you don't have anything to hold the relationship together. Sure, you have something to entertain you, but can it maintain you when hard times come?

If sex was or is your determining factor, then when it is no longer the same, you will run to whatever it is that is going to make it easy for you and to you. That's why we have so many mamas' babies and daddies, maybe because of a one-night stand. Get to know your date before you make that person your mate. The "REALITY" of unnatural love is that it is WRONG! Just because you do not love with the forbidden love, if you are caught in the act of adultery or fornication before you can ask for forgiveness, you are also on your way to HELL!

Now, listen to "REALITY": It is better to try to live the right way than to die living the wrong way. Now I ask you this one question: Are you practicing sin or living sinfully? If you are practicing sin, stop and REPENT now! If you are living sinfully, turn from your wicked ways and REPENT now. God does not want to put you to death. (Ezekiel 33:11: "Say unto them, As I live, saith the Lord GOD, I have no pleasure in the death of the **wicked**; but that the **wicked turn from** his way

THE REALITY OF ABUSE, THE AFTERMATH AND THE RECOVERY

and live: **turn** ye, **turn** ye **from** your evil **ways**; for why will ye die, O house of Israel?") Forbidden love is real, and so is Hell.

I have my forbidden loves too. I am doing everything I can to get it together. I suggest those of you who have forbidden loves do the same.

The thought of going to Hell is a price that I am not willing to pay to continue to live the same way.

Chapter 7
The Art of Giving

Hallelujah, Hallelujah if you know God has been good to you; give God some praise wherever you are!

God is going to bless you so much; you won't have enough room to receive it!

If God has blessed you, stand up on your feet, clap your hands, and shout for joy!

The musicians started playing the shouting music, and people are really praising God, having a Holy-Ghost good time.

I am all smiles thinking it's about time the pastor let God have His way without asking for money. No sooner had I thought this then he, the pastor, turned to the musicians and said, "It's offering time!"

He started saying, "God said 'Bring all the tithes (money) into the storehouse that there may be meat in my house!'" (Mal. 3:10 KJV: "Bring ye all the tithes into the storehouse, that there may be meat in mine house, and prove me now herewith, saith the LORD of hosts, if I will not open you the windows of heaven, and pour you out a blessing, that there shall not be room enough to receive it.")

"Here we go," I said to Shay.

"Sharon, don't start."

"You know I'm gonna start. The Holy Spirit just showed up and not only did the Holy Spirit just show up, Jesus ain't got here yet (*This is the way I felt about the Holy Spirit before I learned better. Thank God I have learned that*

the Holy Spirit is within us and not waiting to show up").
Now here he goes with his faithful saying: 'Bring all the tithes into the storehouse.'

"Who said the storehouse is the church? Especially if the storehouse only takes care of the pastor and his puppeteers?"

"Stop it, Sharon," Shay said while nudging me in the side.

"Whatever!" I said.

I couldn't wait for church to let out. Shay knows I have a mouthful for her to hear. Church finally let out after three hundred or more people brought down their payment on the belief in a miracle or that special blessing the pastor promised God would deliver once they were obedient to the Holy Spirit.

"Wow" was all I could say. God certainly must be looking down in disgust at the mockery of His Word. Walking to the car, I said, "Shay girl, the pastor ought to be ashamed!"

"Oh Lord, here we go; Sharon, do you always have to go to church and find something negative to say just about every time you attend?"

"Shay, you call it negative; I call it wisdom. Not many church-goers can say they have wisdom."

"Okay, Sharon, so what do church-goers have if they don't have wisdom?"

"Girl, they got wisdom, but it's not spelled like the wisdom God gives." She cut me off.

"Sharon, you need to quit. Wisdom can only be spelled one way."

"Nah, not church-goers who don't study the Bible for themselves—they have wis-D-U-M-B." Making sure she understood, I spelled it out for her.

She laughed so hard at me. "Sharon, you are way too much for me."

"Seriously, Shay, when people give their last dime and go home broke, that is truly wis-D-U-M-B! People really need to think about what they do before they do it.

"Pastors, aka Pull-pit Performers, ought to stop pimping God and prostituting Jesus every chance they get, especially on Sunday's."

"How in the world do they pimp God and prostitute Jesus?" Shay asked.

"Easy! They pimp God, telling people He loves a cheerful giver, and prostitute Jesus by saying, 'Give your tithes in Jesus's name, and He will give it back to you.'

"To top things off, after you have given whatever tithe you have to give before church is over, they turn around and say, 'God is telling me someone out here is in need of a miracle or a special blessing.

"'If you know you need God to give you a miracle or that special blessing you've been waiting for, I dare you to sow a seed of one hundred dollars. Come down now! Don't doubt God! Just do it, like Nike! God is faithful and able to do all that you can think or imagine. Come on, come on! Give God what's His anyway!'

"Shay, you know it's true. Even our pastor..., well, your pastor, has done this several times."

"Yes, how can I forget when he does? You constantly nudge me, whispering 'There goes light bill money, gas money, food money, insurance payment money, car note money, school clothes money, babies' diapers money, milk money'; you keep going on using the word *money* time after time until I tell you to shut-up, then you sit looking in amazement at all the people rushing down to give, thinking they are crazy."

"Shay, you are right except for the part where you said I look at times, thinking they are crazy. Take the word *thinking* out because they *are* crazy. I wish I would not give my last dollar to a pimp or prostitute! Thank God, He has given me wisdom and has not allowed Satan's wis-D-U-M-B to affect me."

I leaned over to Shay and asked her, "Have you ever for once stopped to ask yourself, 'What if I don't have any money, but just want special prayer?' what would happen?"

"I don't know, Sharon, but I'm sure you have the answer."

"I may not have the right answer, but I sure would like to know, if in the midst of all their getting money, would they stop and pray for someone who came down without money?

"I'd bet my last dollar they wouldn't stop and pray for someone during this time; it would interfere with their cash flow."

"Sharon, girl, you are out of control. You would gamble away your last dollar just to see, wouldn't you?" Shay said, shaking her head like I was wrong.

"Sho' nuff would. Keep shaking your head at me all you want, but let someone go down there with no money, talking about getting prayer. What they will do is push that person to the side and tell them one of their spiritual leaders will pray with them in the back after church." Before I could finish what I was saying, Shay's mouth dropped open.

"What you got your mouth hanging open for? You know it's true."

Reaching for her purse she got a dollar out and handed it to me.

"What's this for?"

"It's the dollar—your last dollar—you were willing to bet. You won."

I looked at her and started laughing.

"It's not funny, Sharon."

"Why not?"

"Because it happened to me before you and I were truly in need of prayer. They pushed me over to the side and told me exactly what you said."

"Humph, I know they did, and you had to stand there looking at all the people continuing to give their money." I laughed some more and told her, "Girl, you better get some of God's wisdom and leave Satan's wis-D-U-M-B alone."

We both laughed.

"Sharon, you've given me something to think about, but I am not going to let that stop me from giving nor going to church."

"'So long as you give in Jesus' name, He will bless you. That's true, Shay. But the next time you run out of gas coming from church, just remember you put your last dollar in the offering, knowing you needed gas; don't look to God; look to the church.

"Shay, I don't know what's wrong with people giving their light bill money to the church, knowing they have a disconnection notice for the next day. Then they end up sittin' in the dark and can't even call the church for help because they forgot to register as a tithing member; therefore, the church can't help them. Now that's some slick pimpin'."

"Girl, you are a fool!" Shay said, and we both laughed.

"Well, at least I gave you something to think about. While you're thinking about that, think on this too: What good is it for us to go to church every Sunday and sometimes through the week and still live the way we do?"

"What do you mean by that, Sharon?"

"I'm just saying if we as believers go to church for years and don't change, what good is it for us to continue to go?"

"Sharon, God doesn't expect us to be perfect. He just expects us to try to live better" Shay said boldly.

"Live better—that's a nice way of putting it. If you really believe that, you are out of your mind.

"I have sat in service many times in amazement of people's ignorance to the Word of God, until all I heard was the pastor say, "Let us all stand and join hands." Before I could seemingly blink, church was over, and we were on our way out of the church.

"As the ole folk saying goes, "Go into the church a dry Devil; come out a wet Devil!" Guess they knew by the time everyone got through jumping and shouting to the music, they would be wet and sweaty when they came out of the church," I said, just loud enough for Shay to hear me.

"Sharon, you know what?"

"What?"

"I love you in spite of it all."

"I love you, too." I rode silently as Shay drove me to my house.

Shay pulled up to the curb; we gave each other a hug, and Shay said, "Now get your behind out of my car!"

"Okay, I'm getting out, but let me give you some food for thought since we are trying to do better."

Shay looked at me like I was getting on her last nerve. I didn't care because she needed to hear this: "Romans 2:2 KJV says, 'And do not be conformed to this world, but be transformed by the renewing of your mind, that you may prove what *is* that good and acceptable and perfect will of God.'"

"God doesn't expect us to be perfect, but if we do what is in His will we would be better off."

"Yeah, Yeah, Sharon, I hear you. Gotta go now," Shay said.

She darn nearly drove off with my foot still in the car.

All I could do was laugh because sometimes learning the Bible for yourself is hard enough, but trying to share what you've learned about the Bible is even harder.

After reading and learning for myself, I realized that giving is like drawing on a blank canvas—there must be an inspiration behind the picture one puts on the canvas in order for it to be considered art.

Most artists draw because they love expressing themselves without words or expectancy. The only thing the artist expects is for whoever is looking at the picture to draw their own conclusion of what they had to give freely in their art.

After sitting through many church services and watching several (too many) pastors/preachers paint on their canvasses, I rarely saw the beauty within their art. All they did a majority of the time was paint a picture that I had to turn into my own work of art. Therefore, if you have left the church after giving, and your life continues to feel like a blank canvas with nothing but paint on it, then this chapter, "The Art of Giving," may help you turn your life into a work of art.

Let me start by saying Malachi 3:8–10 is a wonderful passage in the Bible. I can truly understand why this is the passage of choice for most church officials to use to encourage the congregation to give tithes (money) to the church.

While it's in the will of God, if you constantly have to quote this Scripture to your congregation in order for them to give, something is terribly wrong. God does not need the money; the church does, but for what purpose?

Perhaps people have gotten away from the real reason why we have churches. Churches should not be a building put together to receive tithes (money) <u>from people but to teach repentance</u> (Matthew 3:1–2 KJV: "[1]In those days came John the Baptist, preaching in the wilderness of Judaea, [2]And saying, Repent ye: for the kingdom of heaven is at hand."),

157

spread the gospel of Jesus Christ (I Corinthians 15:1–4 KJV: "1Moreover, brethren, I declare unto you the gospel which I preached unto you, which also ye have received, and wherein ye stand; 2By which also ye are saved, if ye keep in memory what I preached unto you, unless ye have believed in vain. 3For I delivered unto you first of all that which I also received, how that Christ died for our sins according to the scriptures; 4And that he was buried, and that he rose again the third day according to the scriptures."), and to assemble together in order to encourage and warn one another of the many attacks of Satan and teach that the kingdom of God is at hand (Hebrew 10: 25 NLT: "And let us not neglect our meeting together, as some people do, but encourage and warn each other, especially now that the day of his coming back again is drawing near.").

If you find yourself in a church, preaching only about the blessings of God when you give your tithes, something is terribly wrong once again.

You might need to re-evaluate your church.

I am not saying "Do not tithe"; I am simply saying, you need to give your tithes (money) for the right reason, not because you have been told that God will bless you if you give.

Every time God allows you to see another day in your right mind, that's a blessing.

God is going to bless you no matter what; it's just that the full benefit of God's blessings for you can be shortened.

Why?

Many church officials only draw their focal point on tithes (money), but your blessings can still be short for these reasons: If you have not committed yourself to God completely by the renewing of your mind, your blessings are incomplete. (Rom. 12:1 N LT: "And so, dear brothers and sisters, I plead with you to give your bodies to God. Let them be a living and holy sacrifice—the kind he will accept. When you think of what he has done for you, is this too much to ask?").

If you are only giving and not fasting and praying, you are coming up short on your blessings: [1]Take heed that ye do not your alms before men, to be seen of them: otherwise ye have no reward of your Father which is in heaven... [5]And when thou prayest, thou shalt not be as the hypocrites are: for they love to pray standing in the synagogues and in the corners of the streets, that they may be seen of men. Verily I say unto you, They have their reward. [6]But thou, when thou prayest, enter into thy closet, and when thou hast shut thy door, pray to thy Father which is in secret; and thy Father which seeth in secret shall reward thee openly... [16]Moreover when ye fast, be not, as the hypocrites, of a sad countenance: for they disfigure their faces, that they may appear unto men to fast. Verily I say unto you, They have their reward. [17]But thou, when thou fastest, anoint thine head, and wash thy face; [18]That thou appear not unto men to fast, but unto thy Father which is in secret: and thy Father, which seeth in secret, shall reward thee openly. (Matt. 6:1, 5–6, 16–18 KJV)

Alms simply means money, food, or other donations given to the poor/needy, or anything given as charity. "REALITY" speaks the bottom line: if you are giving tithes (money) because you trust God and not man, then keep on giving.

If you are giving tithes (money) out of duty, then stop, again God does not need you to give tithes (money) because it is His anyway. (Haggai 2:8: "The silver is mine, and the gold is mine, saith the LORD of hosts.").

I challenge all church officials to stop harping on tithes (money) and focus on the real reason for having church, which is to tell all to REPENT (Mark 6:12 NLT: "They went out and preached that people should repent."), not to give.

Please do not misunderstand me, God clearly commands us to give, but if you are not giving cheerfully, God does not need or want your tithes. (2 Corinthians 9:7 KJV: "Every man according as he purposeth in his heart, so let him give; not grudgingly, or of necessity: for God loveth a cheerful giver."). Giving God your pocket change will not do; God is not pleased. What I mean by this is that if you can give more than ten percent, then give it.

I am a living witness to the fact that the more you cheerfully give, the more He gives back to you.

Listen, people of God, if you do not have money to give, give your time to be of service to others. (Galatians 5:13 NLT: "For you have been called to live in freedom—not freedom to satisfy your sinful nature, but freedom to serve one another in love."). If you cannot go and be of service for someone, then fast and pray to God; He will answer your prayers. If you choose not to fast then pray and believe He will answer your prayer/s. However, if your prayers seem to go unanswered, then it's not because God did not hear you, but your faith must be strong and unshakable. You must believe without a doubt:

6 Be careful for nothing; but in everything by prayer and supplication with thanksgiving let your requests be made known unto God. 7 And the peace of God, which passeth all understanding, shall keep your hearts and minds through Christ Jesus. 8 Finally, brethren, whatsoever things are true, whatsoever things are honest, whatsoever things are just, whatsoever things are pure, whatsoever things are lovely, whatsoever things are of good report; if there be any virtue, and if there be any praise, think on these things. 9 Those things, which ye have both learned, and received, and heard, and seen in me, do: and the God of peace shall be with you. (Phil: 4:6-9 KJV) Then what you asked for will be given to you sooner or later. Know that His peace is with you and never doubt Him. He will do it! I know it is hard to believe when you can't see your way when you are in need of something from God, but the only way God can meet your needs is if you believe He will.

I used to pray, expecting God to answer my prayer immediately. I had to learn to believe even though my prayer seemed to remain unanswered.

Before learning better, I would repeat the same prayer every day, still not getting an answer.

I became so frustrated with God I didn't want to read my Bible anymore.

No matter how I tried not to read my Bible, I had to pick it up and read it, hoping to find an answer to my burning question: Why is God not answering prayer?

One day, frustrated, I picked up my Bible, and it fell open to Hebrews. (I have always been one to believe when my Bible falls open on its own, then that must be where God intends for me to start reading).

I began to not only get impatient, but bored too. Just as I was about to stop, I read one last verse: Hebrews 11:1KJV: "Now faith is the substance of things hoped for, the evidence of things not seen." I read this verse over and over again. I knew God had a message for me within this particular verse.

Although I had heard preachers preach using this verse, I never paid attention to the word "Now." However, reading it constantly, all I could focus on was the word "NOW."

Slowly as I read the verse one last time, God gave me my answer as to why it seemed as though my prayer was not getting answered.

There was no need to continue to pray for the same thing. Why pray if every time I finished praying, I continued to hope my prayer would be answered?

Not one time after praying did I get up, walking in the evidence of things unseen. The Holy Spirit revealed to me through this verse by using the word "NOW."

Once I prayed, I was praying in hope, "the substance of things hoped for."

Once I finished praying, I needed to get up with the faith to believe in "the evidence of things unseen."

The reason why my prayers seemed to go unanswered was because I didn't have right "NOW" faith.

I say to you when you pray, don't hope your prayer will be answered; walk having faith in the evidence of the unseen.

"REALITY" showed me that it wasn't until I stopped worrying about what I saw and started believing in what I couldn't see; my prayers then seemed to get answered right away.

As my prayers continue to be answered, my faith continues to grows, and because of my faithfulness (not how much I tithed), God rewards me, making me whole. (Matthew 15:28 KJV: "Then Jesus answered and said unto her, O woman, great is thy faith: be it unto thee even as thou wilt. And her daughter was made whole from that very hour.")

I give tithes or money when He lays it on my heart to give, not because the preacher said to, but because the God in me says to.

People of God, please pay attention to where your money is going.

Especially if your pastor holds an offering for twenty minutes, then afterwards he or she preaches you into generosity, then he turns around and holds the miracle or blessing offering for another thirty minutes yelling and screaming. "Come on, come on, don't miss your blessing!" (You can't miss a blessing that God has for you, because it's for you.) Or, "Don't question God; just do it." (God ain't Nike, so you'd better question your giving.) Or, "Hold your envelopes up so your blessing will come down." (God doesn't come down; He's all around.) My all-time favorite is, "If you don't have cash, put your card number on the envelope." (Will a man rob God? Yes. How so? In tithes and offerings [See Malachi 3:8–12 KJV for the complete context.]). People, if

God has not laid it on your heart to give, keep your money, because God doesn't want you to go "BANKRUPT FOR A BLESSING!"

I have sat in services and watched how preachers patiently wait for (as they say) obedient servants who truly believe, to come down the aisles and drop their money in the bucket; however, they can't stop during this time and pray for people.

It never ceases to amaze me when pastors allow a service to be extended when money is involved. But if the Holy Spirit is moving throughout the church and people are praying for deliverance, the music stops and the people shouting and praying are walked out! (Excuse my church etiquette: the proper name for the ones escorting [walking] the people out are ushers.)

Please again pay attention to where your tithing money goes.

The money that you give in church should be used to meet the needs of those who are "indeed in need." Not for a man who says he is a man of God to get rich quick.

I am astonished when I see pastors driving luxury cars and have members with cars leaking oil or running hot, or they're walking to church in need of a car.

Am I saying that a pastor should not drive a Mercedes?

No!

What I am saying is if your church has the means to provide a way for the pastor to get to church on Sunday, should they not try to provide a way for their members to get back and forth to church safely and meet the needs of their families as well? Am I saying give them transportation?

No!

I'm saying put a program... oops! (Sometimes I forget that I am talking about a church and not a business.) I mean, put a ministry of transportation into place so perhaps these faithful tithers can have a way to continue to pay tithes to the church and not have to stand on the street corners during the blistering heat or the chilling cold weather.

"REALITY": it is hard to convince sinners how wonderful God is, when you are in no better shape than they are; especially, if you're at a bus stop waiting on the same bus as the sinner. There are churches that provide transportation, but they have limitations on transportation.

Is it fair for the man/woman of God to live in a big, lavishly furnished home and have homeless members? Surely this is not the plan God has for His servants.

Am I saying that the man/woman of God should give up what God has blessed them with?

No!

What I am saying is, make sure, before you go and buy the luxuries that you desire with the salary (tithers' money) that the church has given you that you look and make sure your sheep are taken care of beforehand.

You, being the man/woman of God, should get a job so you can afford to live and not be paid by the church, to ensure that the sheep God has placed you over are taken care of.

I know many of you believe that if you are the pastor of a church, this gives you the right to be paid by the church. This is true; however, I prefer to take on the same beliefs as Paul.

In the book of 1 Corinthians, Paul talks about how he would rather die than to lose his distinction of preaching without charge. (1 Corinthians 9:18 KJV: "What is my reward then? Verily that, when I preach the gospel, I may make the gospel of Christ without charge, that I abuse not my power in the gospel.")

Paul also states that since he is not paid by the people then he does not have to preach for the people; he preaches for God: ¹⁰Wasn't he actually speaking to us? Of course he was. Just as farm workers who plow fields and thresh the grain expect a share of the harvest, Christian workers should be paid by those they serve. [11]We have planted good spiritual seed among you. Is it too much to ask, in return, for mere food and clothing? [12]If you support others who preach to you, shouldn't we have an even greater right to be supported? Yet we have never used this right. We would rather put up with anything than put an obstacle in the way of the Good News about Christ. [13]Don't you know that those who work in the Temple get their meals from the food brought to the Temple as offerings? And those who serve at the altar get a share of the sacrificial offerings? [14]In the same way, the Lord gave orders that those who preach the Good News should be supported by those who benefit from it. [15]Yet I have never used any of these rights. And I am not writing this to suggest that I would like to start now. In fact, I would rather die than lose my distinction of preaching without charge. [16]For preaching the Good News is not something I can boast about. I am compelled by God to do it. How terrible for me if I didn't do it! 17If I were doing this of my own free will, then I would deserve payment. But God has chosen me and given me this sacred trust, and I have no choice. 18What then is my pay? It is the satisfaction I get from preaching the Good News without expense to anyone, never demanding my rights as a preacher. 19This means I am not bound to obey people just because they pay me, yet I have become a servant of everyone so that I can bring them to Christ. (1 Cor. 9:10–19 NLT)

For those of you who believe I'm wrong, that's okay; however, I just choose to agree with the Great Theologian, Paul.

On the other hand, "REALITY" also proves that, if the preacher can be paid for preaching, why can't the choir members or the ushers receive pay (reward) from the tithers' money?

Are they not using what God gave them to work in the church?

I know to some it sounds ridiculous to think such a thing.

Well, why not?

Is this not why the members of the churches pay tithes—to take care of the servants of God?

Everybody gets paid except the choir members and the ushers.

Oops! Now-a-days, the professional singers get paid to sing with the choir, but ushers in all my years of going to church have never been known to be paid. I believe if anybody gets paid, the ushers should, because they stand the longest and do the most work. In my experience, musicians get paid, but they sit during the entire service; the minister of music (choir director), who teaches songs mostly known from listening to the radio, gets paid, but stands the same amount of time that the entire choir stands; and the praise and worship leaders get paid to do what the deacons used to do for free. In case you have forgotten, it was once called devotion.

I know many of you believe that these servants, choir members, and ushers should not be paid (even though those with the easiest job and least amount of work in or for the church get paid a salary); because they are not really beneficial to the church, so why pay them? (I am sure these humble servants are not looking to be paid by the church.)

I'll tell you why they should be paid. The church would not be as successful without these servants; for example, there would be no order in the church without the ushers to control the children or the Spirit-filled. (When the Holy Spirit truly enters the body, the spirit-filled are no longer in control, and God takes care of them. However, I'm talking about the ones who are about to run into a wall; they need the ushers to keep them from hurting themselves.)

There would be no one to usher the Holy Spirit in (The Holy Spirit is already present; the choir's singing can at times help one to take their mind off of problems in order for them to feel the presence of the Holy Spirit.), if the choir members did not sing.

Not discounting the praise and worship leaders, members who attend a church with a choir still want to hear the choir sing.

Many who attend church will not admit that they only come to church to see who's in attendance, sit with their friends that they are only able to see on Sundays, or simply to hear the choir sing.

Hardly ever does a non-believer come to church to hear the preacher; ninety-five percent of the time you convince a non-believer to come to church by telling them that someone famous attends or the choir sings well. Non-believer's rarely come to church to hear the preacher; they come seeking someone or to be seen, not to hear the Word of God most of the time.

However, because the choir (through the Holy Spirit) usually softens their hearts, they can receive something from the preached word.

Now, I ask again, "Since tithes are used to pay the preachers for doing what God has called them to do, can the tithes not be used to pay others in the church that are doing what they believe God called them to do?"

Not only are churches monitoring which servants should be paid or how much they pay the pastor, churches are also becoming too concerned and focused on who can build the biggest church, and get on television or radio time the fastest!

These resources to get God's Word out are wonderful to use, however they are primarily used to preach the good news, for a prayer request line, or to talk about prosperity; these resources are rarely used to preach repentance.

I am certain there are some who are preaching repentance; they are just few and far between. Wake up and face "Reality"; just because a man/woman can preach the "feel-good" news (This is what I call sermons that cater more to the congregations feelings versus the word of God) in a big church, on television or radio, or via web, does not mean that God sent them.

Money is what got them the gig. (I use the term *gig* because this is what money pays for in the worldly industry.).

Satan can preach, teach, and reach just as well. Therefore, don't you get fooled by those who say they come in God's name, because demons can masquerade as angels. (2 Corinthians 11:14–15 KJV: "14And no marvel; for Satan himself is transformed into an angel of light.15 Therefore it is no great thing if his ministers also be transformed as the ministers of righteousness; whose end shall be according to their works.") Remember God's "REALITY" check for all who attend church. (Matt. 24:24 KJV: "For there shall arise false

Christs, and false prophets, and shall shew great signs and wonders; insomuch that, if it were possible, they shall deceive the very elect.") However, because God loves us so much, He plainly states "if it were possible," all would be lost. But for those of you who are sitting back waiting on a preacher, teacher, clergyman, priest, bishop, apostle, prophet, evangelist, pope, elder, reverend, pastor or anyone who professes to be called by God to help you pay your way to heaven, you will not get there.

Take this advice from "REALITY": If you do not study and get an understanding for yourself from God, you are in trouble and full of wis-D-U-M-B. (2 Tim. 2:15 KJV: "Study to shew thyself approved unto God, a workman that needeth not to be ashamed, rightly dividing the word of truth.")

I am not saying that one who is called by God cannot direct you, but don't let this be your only way to God. Get the directions, but let God become your guide.

Truthfully speaking, "The Called" one is just that—called—however, you could be the chosen one to turn the world around.

Always remember, many are called, but few are chosen. (Matt. 20:16 KJV: "So the last shall be first, and the first last: for many be called, but few chosen.")

I leave you with this "REALITY," simply because one can say they are called doesn't mean they are CHOSEN!

Chapter 8
The "Pull-pit" Performer

"Oh my goodness," I said, looking at the time. "*I have got to get out of here before my Sunday school class starts.*

"How would it look for the members to be at the church on time and their teacher is late?" I said, chastising myself as I rushed into the car.

It pleased me to be able to teach the class, despite the few seasoned members in my class who were set in their ways of believing.

They also wondered how a youngster could teach them about the Bible.

I recalled one of the older members saying: "I don't know why or how Pas-sa let you teach Sunday school. You ain't knee high to a duck, chile. Lawd how mersay on Pas-sa," she said as she feebly walked away.

I just shook my head and said, "Lord, bless her soul."

"Good morning, my brothers and sisters in Christ. Let's get class started," I said as I looked at the faces of those sitting before me.

"Good morning," they all replied, except the few who didn't approve of me teaching class.

I said a little prayer and continued on with the lesson.

Excited about this particular lesson God had revealed so much to me while studying last night.

The lesson was entitled: "Does God Hear All Prayers?"

For years I had been taught and convinced that God does hear all prayers; He just doesn't answer all prayers. To my surprise, this was the furthest thing from the truth.

Eager to share what was revealed to me, I read the lesson title to the class. After reading the title, I immediately asked: "How many of you believe God hears all prayers?"

Not surprisingly, a majority of the class believed this to be true like I did before studying. Those who did not raise their hands were either beginners in Christ or had no clue.

As I look around, of course, long time member of the church Sista Genesis-to-Revelations (This was my secret name for her because she believed she knew the Bible from beginning to end.) stated the usual: "I been studying the Bible and serving the Lord longer than you' been livin', Chile." She then asked me: "What do you think?"

I looked at her and confidently said: "No."

Her mouth dropped open like she had a sudden case of lock-jaw, but of course she recovered quickly.

She replied with confidence, authority and power: "God does hear all prayers. He may not answer them, but He mos' de-fan-eat-ly hear'em."

I have to break her words into syllables to make out the word she was trying to say. She constantly tries to use words bigger than her vocabulary. I laugh on the inside thinking, *"No she ain't trying to go there!"* Broken grammar and mispronounced words and all; she proudly challenges me every time I teach class.

This is one Sunday I was not going to take the high road. She's going to be one hot and mad Sista today. She will not bully me around. The Bible will be my weapon today and not my attitude.

Therefore, I knew our pastor was going to get an earful after class.

"Thank you, Sister, for sharing with us your words of wisdom this morning," I said, hoping she would sit down and be quiet.

She gave me her nod of assurance with chest poked out, as if to say, "Don't challenge me on this either."

"Ump! By the time I finish with you Sista girl you gon' look real stupid. Lord let me not go there," talking to myself.

I took a deep breath and said: "Let's open our Bibles and see what the Word has to say about our topic. If you will, please turn to Isaiah 59:1–2 King James Version (I always stated the Bible version I would be reading from because Sista Genesis-to-Revelations would ask: "Wha' var-shon you readin'?"). It reads: 'Behold, the LORD's hand is not shortened, that it cannot save; neither his ear heavy, that it cannot hear: 2 But your iniquities have separated between you and your God, and your sins have hid his face from you, that he will not hear.'"

Looking up at the class, I asked "Why is it that God allowed Isaiah to write this in the Bible, if God heard all prayers?"

I scanned the classroom to see who had an answer to my question; no one said anything.

Just as I was about to give my explanation, Sista Genesis-to-Revelations said: "God can hear the prayer; He just not going to answer the prayer."

"Yes Ma'am, I do believe God can hear all, but when we as believers live sinfully and expect God to answer our prayers without our asking for forgiveness, we are praying in vain. Remember, without repentance, sin will shorten His hand (hid His face) and He will not hear us."

Before she could open her mouth, I said: "Quick question: How many of you have experienced talking with someone, and when they ask you to repeat what was said, you have to ask them to repeat what they just said to you? Your body may have been there, but your ears heard nothing that was said."

Every hand went up except that of Sista Genesis-to-Revelations.

My point exactly. God is present everywhere, and still He will not hear you because of your sins. (I guess she saw no way around what I said, so she sat through the rest of class, madder than a junkyard dog chasing a thief.)

"The only prayer God hears from a sinner is a prayer of repentance.

"Let me give you an example: if I were to pray and ask God for two kilos of cocaine, and I miraculously received two kilos of cocaine, do you believe God answered my prayer?"

The classroom was completely silent.

Once again, when I was about to explain, Sista Genesis-to-Revelations said, "God could have given you the cocaine to teach you a lesson."

("Jesus, you better hold my tongue because she has me beyond .38 hot; I'm .44 hot, and she better recognize I ain't always been saved. I will put Jesus down; go toe to toe with her fat behind up in here! Lord, please forgive me; you know I am sick of her!" I was trying not to show my disgust of how ignorant I thought she was and sounded.*)*

"Ump, ump," I said, clearing my throat and gathering my composure before I opened my mouth to speak. "Again, thank you Sister, for your input.

"You have a point; I could have gotten the cocaine, but would God answer a prayer giving me something that would cause nothing but chaos and confusion?

"Let's be realistic; we all know that drugs lead to violence, addiction, and crime." Without pausing, I said, "Turn to 1 Corinthians 14:33; it reads: 'For God is not the author of confusion, but of peace, as in all churches of the saints.' For you Bible scholars, I know Paul was talking about the order in which church should be conducted; however, the Scripture clearly states: 'God is not the author of confusion.'

"When we watch the news or watch any movie that has drugs associated with it, we see nothing but chaos and confusion."

Looking around, I could see those who understood what I was saying were nodding their heads in agreement. However, there were a few nod-less heads adamant about believing God does hear all prayers; He just doesn't answer them, even though the Scripture clearly states He will not hear them.

Believing I had proven beyond doubt the answer to the Sunday school lesson topic, I heard: "The question is 'Does God hear all prayers,' not 'Was He the author of confusion?'"

Of course, the person saying this was Sista Genesis-to-Revelations. She is working my last nerve, never sittin' over there takin' up a whole bench lookin' like a big Silverback Gorilla. Just like a gorilla when they need to be seen and not heard, they are always loud, wrong, and out of order.

"Lord, please forgive me for my thoughts, but she does look like a gorilla and looks stinky too! Lord, I know I'm wrong. Help me."

I could not believe her determination.

"Yes, you are right; the question was not 'Is God the author of confusion,' but when you ask God through prayer for something that is clearly going to cause confusion, God is not going to answer because He is not listening for foolishness. Turn to Proverbs 24:9 it reads: 'The thought of foolishness is sin: and the scorner is an abomination to men.'

"Is asking God for cocaine not foolishness?

"Did the Scripture not say, 'the thought of foolishness is sin?'?"

Before she could respond, the Superintendent of Sunday School came into the sanctuary and said that it was time for all classes to combine into one to hear the Pastors overview of the lesson.

"Thank you all for listening, and may God bless us all. Amen." And I closed my Bible to head to my seat.

The classroom erupted in applause.

I was so shocked!

On my way to sit down, several of the classroom attendees shook my hand saying, "God is really using you."

I smiled and politely said, "I certainly hope so."

The Pastor came out of the pastor's study and gave his overview of the lesson, prayed, and dismissed Sunday School.

Sunday School always ended fifteen minutes before the morning service was to start.

During the fifteen minutes, members who did not attend Sunday School would arrive, joining the ones who did attend Sunday School in the church's café to fellowship while having donuts and coffee before the morning worship service.

While having coffee, several members continued to compliment me on how well the lesson was taught and how I gave them something more to research.

I was elated that they were willing to go and research the Scriptures more, and perhaps soon share some of their knowledge and wisdom with me.

Tossing my coffee cup into the garbage, I went into the sanctuary and waited for the service to start.

Sitting down in my usual seat, I could see Sista Genesis-to-Revelations talking to the pastor.

Once they finished talking, she looked directly at me with a mean mug smirk (the look people give you when you walk past them) on her face, looking identical to a mother gorilla protecting her baby she carried around from harm.

Assuming she discussed the lesson with the pastor, by the mean mug smirk she gave me, he either agreed with her or at least found a way to put her at ease regarding the lesson.

By the time pastor got through preaching, I was left with the "Pull-pit Blues."

His sermon started out wonderfully, although by the time he was done, it sounded more like his own personal message rather than God's.

193

He (not God) went on and on about how believers whom God put in a position to share the Word must be careful not to misinterpret the Scriptures.

The entire time he was preaching, Sista Genesis-to-Revelations, aka Silverback Gorilla, was whooping and hollering, "Preach yo preach, Preacha!"

I was saying to myself, *"That's exactly what he's doing—preaching his preaching and not God's preaching."*

Disappointed, I thought, *"How could he allow himself to be manipulated into preaching such a sermon?"*

Satan is so crafty!

Not wanting Satan to have victory over me, I said: "Oh well, to God be the glory."

Maybe someone needed to hear the sermon.

This is how I made myself believe the sermon was not about what went on in the Sunday School class that morning.

Once pastor dismissed the service, he said: "Sis. Sharon, I need to see you in my office for a brief moment, please."

Right then and there, I knew without a doubt his sermon was meant for me and only me.

"Sure, Pastor, I'll meet you in your office."

Once in his office he asked me to have a seat.

Sitting down quickly, I was eager to get this meeting over with.

He looked at me and asked: "Sister Sharon, how was your class this morning?"

"Class was wonderful!"

"That's good."

Awkward silence for a moment; then, he said, "Sister Sharon, it's been kinda hard lately having two Sunday School teachers teaching the same class. Last Sunday proved to me just how confusing it can get."

"Why, Pastor? I teach every 1st, 3rd and 5th Sunday." I was not confused at all.

"Last Sunday, Sis. Bertha was not here and neither were you."

"Pastor, you know that I go visit my son in prison on the Sunday's that I am not responsible for teaching."

"Yes I know, but you still have a commitment as a Sunday School teacher."

I could not believe I was sitting here listening to him make up excuses to have me step down as a teacher all because Sis. Bretha couldn't keep her end of our commitment (this was my assumption of his going on and on about the Sunday's Sis. Bertha missed).

Pastor knew she wasn't an in-depth studier of the Bible in the first place. She wasn't even committed to attending church regularly enough to have been put in such an important position.

I hate it when people try to insult my intelligence, and this is exactly what Pastor was sitting here doing.

I said nothing to him. I sat in complete silence.

He was going to have to ask me to step down. I was not about to make this easy for him by suggesting that I step down.

He inhaled deeply and said: "Since there has been so much confusion with this class, and now because people have been complaining about the confusion amongst the teachers (I know he's not trying to blame me. *"Wow"*, is all I thought.), I think its best that I combine the classes into one until we can get a commitment from a member who can be here every Sunday."

"Okay Pastor, not a problem."

He sat there for a minute and finally asked, "Is that all you have to say?"

"Yes Sir. You are the pastor, and all I can do is be obedient."

"Sista Sharon, thank you for understanding," he said while breathing a sigh of relief.

"Well I guess this concludes our meeting," Pastor said, popping up, like a piece of toast fresh out of the toaster to shake my hand.

"Okay, Pastor, you have a good evening," I said as I walked out of his office in disbelief, because I never thought in a million years that my pastor would become what I call a "Pull-pit Performer" (title I use for pastors who are puppets).

My definition of a "Pull-pit Performer": Individuals who profess that God has called them to represent Him in the pulpit, but they pull you into a pit of misguided teachings becoming a performer for the members instead of God.

When God has called someone to the pulpit, it is not about them, it is about God. The "Pull-pit Performer's" main objective is to make an impression on man while expressing the word of God in such a way that they benefit from their own teaching.

"Wow" again, was all I could say. I gathered my things and headed home, glad to be done with teaching the class.

Even though I loved teaching, I wanted to quit a long time ago. Having to look at the aggravated faces of those who thought they knew the Bible better than the ones who wrote the Bible was sickening.

It didn't take me long to look past them, since my teaching was not about me or them, only about the Word of God, which was my sole purpose for teaching. This was the rationale I used to convince myself not to quit teaching.

Little good did my rationale do; I was still asked to quit, all because a faithful, large tithe-payer had a problem with me.

This was the eye-opener for me with that church. It's cool for you to make all the sacrifices as long as you do what the big bankers (tithers) say. If not, you will surely be pushed swiftly to the side or outside the church.

I've heard many stories of the importance of tithing, but never had I experienced the "Big Tithing Bullies." That's right; there are not only bullies outside of the church, they are inside, sitting on the front row, bullying pastors.

Because of their money, they have the power to dictate and control pastors.

Not all pastors are bullied; some are greedy and want the Big Tithing Bullies' money. Therefore, they make what these tithers want as their own priority instead of allowing God's will to be done.

The Deacons Committee keeps the pastor informed of who gives the most money and how often they pay tithes.

In turn the deacons' loyalty is rewarded with power to be the pastor's right-hand man, and in huge churches this is a position worth fighting for.

They get the benefits of money, recognition, first-class treatment, women (in some cases men), five-star hotels, and whatever luxuries come with being the mega churches' pastors' right-hand men.

The "Big Tithing Bullies" (BTB) and the "Right Hand Man" (RHM) have mastered the "Art of Giving"; they know how to give what they want and do what they need to do to get what they need done. They give and do more than enough to get the power they need in order to control the pastors' sermons as well as the church operations—who does what, when, and where.

The "BTB" gives the money and the "RHM" gives the information.

These masters of giving are some of the worst members for a pastor to have within his congregation. The pastor becomes their prey, because they determine his salary, when he gets paid, the directions of his sermons, and when his money is in jeopardy.

Since many pastors have adjusted his/her lifestyle based on the money they are paid by the church, they now have to do what the "BTB" and the "RHM" expect.

These individuals are the ones who really run the church because they are big-tithe payers, and large portions of the money they give contribute to the pastor's salary and not the successful operations of the church.

News flash, "Pull-pit Performer," God doesn't need their money and neither do you! He is the Creator of individuals who came up with the concept of currency; therefore He will supply you with what you need.

Oh I truly understand how this happens, because for centuries we have been taught the "Art of Giving" by "Pull-Pit Performers." And this method of teaching has been passed on generation after generation.

I have been told since I can remember that the best way to receive from God is to give tithes. Therefore, I have made it my lifestyle.

Until I learned to study the Bible for myself, I was developed by the "Pull-pit Performer" to believe his interpretation of tithing, due to the "Pull-pit Performer's" favorite quote: "The more you give God, the more He gives to you."

I treated tithing like a slot machine—if I put in twenty-five dollars, I expected at least a hundred dollars back. I'm laughing to myself, saying, *"Yes ma'am, you did!"*

Because of my developmental mindset, tithing created a change in my lifestyle. I gave money I didn't have because the "Pull-pit Performer" assured me that God was going to give me it back.

After many days of hunger and nights of darkness (due to lights being cut off), I began to rethink my giving.

In spite of what I had been told and taught, I learned that giving money and expecting God to give me more in return, didn't always happen, leading me to conclude the "Pull-pit Performer" wasn't quite right.

I started studying about tithes and realized that the purpose of tithing is obedience. (1 Samuel 15:22 KJV: "And Samuel said, Hath the Lord as great delight in burnt offerings and sacrifices, as in obeying the voice of the Lord? Behold, to obey is better than sacrifice, and to hearken than the fat of rams.")

My developmental lifestyle teachings from the "Pulpit Performer" taught me that when I gave out of obedience, and it was a sacrifice, God was really going to bless me.

However, my interpretation of the Scripture tells me that sacrifice was not as important if I was not being obedient to God's Word.

Many times when I gave tithes, I gave out of tradition and pressure of expectation, not out of obedience.

Most of the time I gave, I sacrificed my own necessities.

In my heart I knew I was paying my tithe begrudgingly and was not cheerfully giving most of the time.

The Scripture helped me erase what I had been developmentally taught for years regarding tithes. 2 Corinthians 9:7 KJV: "Every man according as he purposeth in his heart, so let him give: not grudgingly, or of necessity: for God loveth a cheerful giver."

Since I loved to give, why did I not love giving to the church?

"REALITY" showed me that my tithes did not always have to go to the church where the "Pull-pit Performer" taught me.

When I would give to those who were in need, I was tithing; when I took time out to see about the elderly, I was tithing; when I stopped to volunteer my services, I was tithing; and when I cleaned the church, it was a tithe.

After getting God's wisdom about tithing, I tithe according to how He has blessed me and I give freely and cheerfully whether it is to the church, helping the elderly, the homeless or a child in need. In whatever way, I give without questioning my giving.

Therefore, I say to you, if you give and question your giving, don't give. Pray and ask God to help you understand the beauty of being able to freely and cheerfully give your tithes and time.

I promise you when you give righteously, you will never have to beg or go without. (Psalm 37:25: "I have been young, and now am old; yet have I not seen the righteous forsaken, nor his seed begging bread.")

Because of my obedience, I can take delight in what His Word says—He will supply all my need (Philippians 4:19: "But my God shall supply all your need according to his riches in glory by Christ Jesus."), which isn't always money.

I "NOW" tithe and make whatever sacrifices I need to for God, expecting nothing in return.

Give out of obedience to the Word of God, not out of bribery from the mouth of the "Pull-pit Performer."

For years, my lack of understanding tithing lead me to sit in church services believing as long as I gave my tithes (ten percent only) God would always give to me more in return.

Now that I understand God's purpose of tithing (not the "Pull-pit Performer' purpose) I see God's blessings come in many ways. Whether the blessing is money, the air that I breathe, being able to wake up, walk, talk, think or simply having the ability to smile is God's blessing in return for my obedience and sacrifice(s).

Please don't get me wrong. I went through many trials before I got to giving out of obedience or sacrifice.

In my earlier years when I asked God for something and didn't get it, I started complaining and whining out of anger because God had not delivered. I was so angry with God that I started being stingy towards people. This was totally out of character for me; I was a natural-born giver (before Christ) not a born again giver (after Christ).

"REALITY" showed up and snapped me back into character. Stopping at Dollar General (a local store), a man who appeared to be homeless was standing near the entrance. I got out of my car with a no-spare-change attitude. The look on my face should have told him not to bother asking, but he did anyway.

"Excuse me, Ma'am. Do you have a dollar to spare in order for me to get something to eat?"

Naturally I said I didn't have anything.

He looked at me and said, "God bless you anyway."

"Thank you. God bless you, too," I said to him in return, as I dashed into the store to escape his broken spirit.

Something came over me; I stood there ashamed, knowing I had a car full of change. I could have at least bought the man something to eat.

To my surprise, he was still there. Judging him, I figured he'd walk on to the next person.

Just as I was about to get in my car, he said: "In spite of it all, I am still grateful."

I turned and said: "Grateful for being hungry?"

"Oh yes, Ma'am! I am alive and able to say I'm hungry."

"I guess that's a good way to see life."

"Yep it is. I was nearly killed two days ago. If all I have to worry about today is something to eat, I am grateful. God blessed me to live another day. I am thankful to be here breathing."

"I know that's right! If you want to go over to McDonald's, I will buy you something to eat."

"Really!?" His eyes lit up like a glow worm.

"Really!" I found myself just as excited.

We got into McDonald's, and he asked for a Mac-double from the dollar menu.

I stepped in and said, "Give him a deluxe meal."

He was in shock. "Oh my goodness, you don't have to spend that kind of money on me. I ain't that special."

I looked at him almost in tears. His deep blue eyes were absolutely beautiful.

"You may not be special to anyone else, but you are special to me because you showed me how to be grateful for what I have."

"Oh yes, Ma'am, no matter what, you should always be grateful, because there is always someone who would love to be in your shoes."

Wow! Did he just quote the exact words of the song I used to sing constantly? (Be Grateful by Walter Hawkins.)

I turned and handed him his order. "Do you mind if I give you a hug?"

"Ma'am, I am homeless and haven't had a bath in a few days. I may not smell too good."

"I'm sure I have smelled worse." With that being said, I hugged him and left him there with a smile.

However, he rushed behind me and said, "Ma'am you made me see the beauty of being able to live a little while longer. You have made my week. May God bless and keep you. Amen."

I smiled and said, "Same to you."

I made it home and became overwhelmed with joy.

"Thank You, Lord. Thank You, Lord, for all You've done for me."

I felt like I had tithed a million dollars to Him.

When you cheerfully give, this is how you should be left feeling. I don't care if it's a penny, if you gave it cheerfully, God is very pleased. (Luke 21:1–4 KJV: "And he looked up, and saw the rich men casting their gifts into the treasury. 2And he saw also a certain poor widow casting in thither two mites. 3And he said, Of a truth I say unto you, that this poor widow hath cast in more than they all: 4For all these have of their abundance cast in unto the offerings of God: but she of her penury hath cast in all the living that she had.")

God continued to show me His reward for my obedience and sacrifice. Not long after the conversation with the man at Dollar General, God clarified to me why the man said he was "grateful to be alive to say I am hungry." I had a major car wreck. My car went across four lanes of traffic during rush hour, hit the divider, went up on two wheels and came down, spinning out of control; it went back across the highway on two wheels and finally landed in the ditch. Miraculously, I hit no one and walked away without a scratch, not even a broken bone.

It was during and after my recovery that I saw how my giving was repaid by God. He gave my strength and health back that I took for granted every day. Understanding this has made me a better person, a big giver and sacrificing to whoever is in need of my time.

I urge you to study the Bible.

No matter how well the "Pull-pit Performer" flatters you with his word, don't fall for it. (Daniel 11:32 KJV: "And such as do wickedly against the covenant shall he corrupt by flatteries: but the people that do know their God shall be strong, and do exploits.")

Don't become a "BTB" just to become an "RHM"; give out of obedience and sacrifice freely without expectancy.

"REALITY": "Pull-pit Performer, I encourage you to stop asking for tithes. Teach your members to become cheerful givers and I promise you, you won't have to preach for the people, deal with the cattiness of members, or worry about the lights staying on. (**S**)lick (**W**)ords (**A**)in't (**G**)od!"

Chapter 9
Holy-Rollers

M y, My, My how can we not see the Holy-Rollers (show offs who come to church dress to impress and give to expect) sitting in "the Amen Corner." I am so tired of going to church, watching the Holy-Rollers sitting, standing in corners gossiping, and turning their noses down at those who are really seeking God in church. "Sit down and shut up!"

"Pull-pit Performers (King of the Holy Rollers), I write in defense of why you perform.

"Listen, if you are giving your tithes (money); thank you very much!

"He, the Performer, will put it to good use.

"Holy Rollers, if you are giving to get a special seat at the church, its working, but keep in mind 'Ain't no special seats in Heaven!'"

Sadly, there is a lot of this going on in churches; it is truly a mockery of God.

God does not care how well you dress or how much you give in tithes (money). He only cares about the souls you have led to Him.

When celebrity Holy Rollers attend church service, you must "only" protect them from the public (fans are fans and they will take any opportunity to get an autograph) without compromising the credibility of God's Word.

Members who are not celebrities should not be receiving preferential treatment, no matter how much they contribute in tithes and/or offerings. (And the pastor should not know who contributes what when.)

Tradition has it that Deacons and Deaconettes (wives of Deacons) are seated on the first two rows anytime a church service is held.

This may have been started with good intentions to display respect, because they worked hand–in-hand with the pastor of the church.

However, what started out as a form of respect is now disrespected by most celebrity guests and those who serve as Deacons/Deaconettes.

Celebrities will walk in late to ensure their name is mentioned, to make sure they are seen, simply because they know they don't have to worry about finding a seat or a parking space.

Many Deacons use this position as power up (meaning the Deacon/s get to make decisions concerning the church and the Pastor allows it in order to keep his secrets hidden) in the church. They (Deacon's) are now privy to have secret extra-marital affairs, because women who are married to them like the prestige of being their wives, and the other women like the thought of becoming the wife.

According to the Bible, a Deacon is supposed to be married and committed to his wife and children, not committed to another woman or sideline kids (kids by someone other than their wife) (1 Timothy 3:12 KJV: "Let the deacons be the husbands of one wife, ruling their children and their own houses well.") in order to be a Deacon.

Unfortunately, the Word of God has been tainted by the Holy-Rollers. They use the Word of God to remain in unfavorable, godless positions and relationships.

The way the church family is allowing things to go on I am not sure if the marital status or morality of a Deacon matters anymore.

Sad but true.

The wives (Princesses of the Holy Rollers) of Deacons hide behind the Word of God and pretend that they have "NO" idea about what their ho'sband (oops, husband) is doing.

Stop the (**_S_**)ittin' (**_E_**)legantly (**_C_**)alm, (**_R_**)idiculously (**_E_**)xpecting (**_T_**)riumph.

I am not saying God can't change things, but if you think He is going to fix your charade, He's not!

He will expose the situation and force you to stop your pretending. So Princess Holy-Roller, get some sense and stop the nonsense!

I refuse to sit and be a Holy-Roller and allow my relationship with Christ to be tainted because I want to pretend my life is perfect. Hello, are you listening?

No one has a perfect life, because we live in a world of imperfection!

I would suggest to the "Pull"-pit Performer's wife, Queen of the Holy-Rollers, to stop the nonsense and get real, too!

Back to the other major problem in the church for the "Pull-pit Performer": preferential seating.

This needs to be, and should be, stopped due to those who take advantage of this privilege. It also has allowed Satan a doorway to cause continued dissention amongst members within the house of God.

I understand "protecting the celebrities" (Heaven has "NO" celebrities!), but they need to know that if they think they can roll up forty-five minutes after service has started and get protection, it AIN'T HAPPENIN'!

They may be a celebrity here on earth, but in God's eyes they are not any different from ordinary people. These Holy-Rollers need to know accountability and respect are God's requirements, not their money.

Perhaps the "Pull-pit Performer" does not want to offend these Holy-Rollers because they contribute a great deal of money to the church.

If this is the case, what does it matter, because if God gave you the vision for the church, He will certainly make the necessary provision for you to run the church!

"Pull-pit Performer," here is a Scripture that should give you the holy boldness you need to **stop tap-dancing** around Holy-Roller members.

Luke 12:24 KJV reads: "Consider the ravens: for they neither sow nor reap; which neither have storehouse nor barn; and God feedeth them: how much more are ye better than the fowls?"

Warning to "Pull-pit Performers": you will be held accountable for the Holy-Rollers' souls.

If the Holy-Rollers' wish to remain a mess, they need to be ousted from the church congregation.

Yes, I said, ousted from the church!

Holy-Rollers' are the reasons why the "Pull-pit Performers" can continue performing.

How can Christians, not Holy-Rollers', expect the church to convert the world if so much of the world is converting the church?

Why do I say this?

When I attend church now–a-days, I don't know if I should say Pass the Patron (ultra-premium Tequila) or Praise the Lord, play or pray, shout or shake it, clap or snap, when the music starts.

What's going on in the church today is out of control!

Why?

Because the "Pull-pit Performers" are too busy performing to fatten their wallets instead of preaching, and the Holy-Rollers' are too busy pretending and not praying.

Both are caught up in their own personal self-praise.

The "Pull-pit Performer" is pleasingly praising the Holy-Rollers' while Holy-Rollers' are pleasantly praising the "Pull-pit Performer," because they tilt the tithing plate, padding it with lots of cash, nonetheless they both are praising for show.

Okay now, for you Holy-Rollers', who are quick to knowingly allow the "Pull-pit Performer" to openly do that which is not of God (knowing the "Pull"-pit Performer" is married and having an affair with someone other than his wife), read carefully! God is not pleased!

The Bible clearly states if you see that your brother is doing wrong and you go along with it, you are a partaker in his evil deeds. (2 John 9–11 KJV: "9 Whosoever transgresseth, and abideth not in the doctrine of Christ, hath not God. He that abideth in the doctrine of Christ, he hath both the Father and the Son.10 If there come any unto you, and bring not this doctrine, receive him not into your house, neither bid him God speed: 11 For he that biddeth him God speed is partaker of his evil deeds.").

"Pull-pit Performer," it is time to stop using Matthew 7:1 KJV ("Judge not that ye be not judged.") as an excuse to continue in evil deeds while overlooking the wrong doings of Holy-Rollers'.

The reason why both the "Pull-pit Performers" and the Holy-Rollers' get away with using the Bible to excuse sinful behavior is because they only read the Scripture beneficial to their situation or read only part of the Scripture.

According to the KJV, Matthew 7:1 does clearly tell us to "judge not, that ye be not judged"; however, if you continue to read to verse 5, remember to make sure you have "the beam out of thine own eye; and then shalt thou see clearly to cast the mote out of thy brother's eye." Keep in mind when correcting your brother or sister to let it be done in love (1 Cor. 16:14 KJV: "Let all that you do be done in love.").

This is not judging, this is the truth!

"Pull-pit Performer," you are simply telling the Holy-Rollers', if they do not turn from their wicked ways, they will not make it to heaven.

"Pull-pit Performer," don't twist God's Word; if you are doing the same thing/s as the Holy-Rollers' and have not gotten the plank out of your own eye, you are a hypocrite. (Matthew 7:5 KJV: "Thou hypocrite, first cast out the beam out of thine own eye; and then shalt thou see clearly to cast out the mote out of thy brother's eye.")

Matthew 15:7–9 KJV speaks clearly to the "Pull-pit Performers" and the Holy-Rollers'. It reads:

7 "Ye hypocrites, well did Esaias prophesy of you, saying, 8 This people draweth nigh unto me with their mouth, and honoureth me with their lips; but their heart is far from me. 9 But in vain they do worship me, teaching for doctrines the commandments of men."

"REALITY": if you ain't real, **step down** from the pulpit, "Pull-pit Performer," or **step out** of the church, Holy-Roller'!

Chapter 10
Forgiveness

"God! How much more must I endure?" I had to fight to keep my sanity, survive the brutal denial of my family regarding my abuse, sit back and watch my abuser live as though he was the one violated, and now my nephew tells me of his abuse horror!

"Why me, Lord?" I've gone through the fire of abuse. I stopped, dropped, and let it all roll over me.

When will the backdraft of abuse cease?

I'm tired, hurt, drained, devastated, demoralized, and fed up with all this mess! I ain't taking no more! I'm not forgiving or excusing anyone else. This is the last straw!

My phone kept ringing.

I'm in my moment of pain. Who in the world keeps ringing my phone?

I glance at the number, didn't recognize it, so I pushed ignore.

Getting back to my rampage at God,... the phone rings again and again.

It's that same number.

Tired of whoever it was calling, I answered: "Hello."

"Hello sweetheart, how are you?"

"Fine, how are you?" I did not want to take my anger out on whoever this was on the other end of the line.

"I am blessed."

"That's good. May I ask who I am speaking with?"

"Oh sweetheart, I am sorry. This is Sis. Daniels. The little short lady you met a while back during a conference in which you spoke. We chatted while waiting for others to return from lunch."

"Oh yes, Sis. Daniels, I remember you. We hit it off right away."

"Yes, we did.

"Do you recall giving me your number?"

"Yes."

"Wonderful!

"The Lord laid you in my spirit this morning, and I just called to pray with you."

Shocked by her words, I just held the phone.

"Sweetheart, are you still there?"

"Yes, Ma'am."

"Good. I thought I lost you. You know how these cellphones will drop a call."

"Yes Ma'am, I do."

"I didn't call to keep you long. I just want to be obedient to the Holy Spirit.

"Let me pray real quickly for you."

"Oh Lord, here we go!" I said to myself. "Yes, Ma'am," I said while rolling my eyes upward.

"Father, I come to YOU this morning in the humblest way I know how, asking you to cleanse me of my sins and forgive me for anything that I may have done that is not pleasing to YOU.

"Father God, I come before you on behalf of Sis. Sharon. Lord, I don't know YOUR plans for her life, but YOU do. I come asking that she opens up her heart to be a willing vessel; she may not understand YOUR will or YOUR way.

"Lord, renew her mind to understand (that) YOU are in control of her life. Help her surrender it all unto YOU.

"Father God, I don't know what it is that has her heart so heavy, but YOU do. I ask that YOU break the cycle that is binding her up."

(I was just letting her pray to hurry and get off the phone, but when she said, "Break the cycle," I began to feel the presence of God.)

"Let her open up her heart to forgive those who have unjustly wronged her. Let her see that forgiveness is the only way she can be forgiven. Let her harden not her heart.

"Let YOUR grace and mercy reign over her. Father! This is YOUR child! Let her know that YOU are with her always.

"When the Devil comes her way, cut him off and cast him back into the gates of Hell where he belongs!

"Father God, YOU are the author and finisher of her! She will surrender to YOU!

"I come in holy boldness, commanding Satan to take his hands off YOUR child!

(Tears started to flow like never before. My nose was running, my hands were trembling and I began to say: *"Yes Lord, Yes to YOUR way."*)

"Father God, forgive her for her sins.

"Let her know forgiveness is the key to healing. Remove all the hurt, bitterness, anger, distrust and hatred which may have penetrated her spirit. Restore her joy back. Purge her. Cleanse her with hyssop.

"Father God, we thank YOU in the Mighty name of Jesus, giving YOU all the praise and the glory. Amen and Amen."

"Hallelujah! Hallelujah! Thank you, Jesus! Father, forgive me! I surrender all to YOU! Use me Lord! I am your child! Hallelujah! Hallelujah! Thank you Jesus!" I rejoiced!

"Yes, yes chile, surrender it all to HIM. Let go and let God."

"Yes Lord! Yes to YOUR will! Yes to YOUR way! I give it all to YOU! Oh God, thank YOU! Thank YOU Jesus, thank YOU Jesus!" Tears continued flowing.

"Yes, yes, yes Lord. Let it all out. Thank you Father God! Release! Release!

"In the mighty name of Jesus, I command you, Satan, to flee!" Sis. Daniels cried out.

"Oh God, I'm sorry; please, forgive me!" I screamed loudly.

"Peace, be still," Sis. Daniels softly spoke.

Suddenly, I became so relaxed. The fear, the panic, and the pain were gone.

"Sis. Daniels, how can I thank you?"

"Sweetheart, I was only obeying the Lord. No thanks needed. You be about our Father's business. Take care."

Just like that she hung up. I looked at the phone in complete amazement as I put the phone back on the receiver; I was still amazed by Sis. Daniels. In spite of the powerful prayer, my emotions were aloof and my mental anguish continued. I needed to calm down so I went into the bathroom and turned on the shower.

As I slowly got undressed, it was as if I were on autopilot. I reached under the bathroom sink and grabbed a disposal douche, prepared to follow my three-step ritual:

Step one: I turned on the hot water, allowing the temperature to get a few degrees before scalding, and stood there for five to ten minutes, allowing the water to pre-rinse the first layer of pain away.

Step two: I lathered my towel with soap and began scrubbing my skin feverishly until the invisible touch of my abuser's hands seemingly washed away.

Step three: I rinsed my insides with the disposal douche repeatedly in order to feel clean. This in my mind erased the vulnerability I felt as a child after being raped. Because I was so young at the time, I had no way to feel completely clean on the inside other than to take a bath. Taking a bath helped, but when I learned about douching I tried it, and the clean sensation I got was the cloak and dagger

I needed to rinse away the imaginary bodily fluids he left with me.

Every time I finished my three-step ritual I said: *"You have to stop this. It can't be healthy for your body."*

Although it had been over twenty years ago, I still could not mentally stop my three-step ritual. It was my way of coping with the unclean feeling I felt since the first time my abuser completely raped me.

Back to the matter at hand: getting in the shower; just as I was about to jump in, something came over me.

I had the sudden urge to take a bath.

A bath? There's no way. I hadn't taken a bath in years.

Taking a bath meant I would have to relive my experiences as a child.

To take a bath then was not only a fight, but a challenge. Instantly I was having flashbacks of how much bubble bath or dishwashing liquid I used to put in the water to cover the smell of my Step-Daddy's cologne combined with stale, cigarette breath mixed with day-old beer.

"God really, YOU want me to take a bath?"

I can't. I won't. Am not!

In a complete panic, I became frantic—almost hysterical. I immediately turned the water off and reached for the door knob to open up the bathroom door, but I couldn't get it to open. I turned and pulled to no avail; the door would not open!

"God why, why?"

I leaned over the toilet because panic had set in so bad, I needed to throw up.

Trying to get the lid raised, I knocked over the décor on the toilet tank, which had a Bible on it.

Dang it!

As I reached to pick up the décor, my eyes locked in on the Bible.

It was open.

I looked at the verse; it read: "Trust in the Lord with all thine heart; and lean not unto thine own understanding. In all thy ways acknowledge him, and he shall direct thy paths" (Pro. 3:5–6KJV).

I wanted to continue reading, but it was like all the other words had become a blur.

I sat there reading the verse repeatedly. I knew the verse by heart because I had quoted it word-for-word to many who were in doubt of God.

It was at this time that I could see how easy it was to quote Scriptures, but extremely hard to follow them.

I love God with all my heart; albeit a struggle, I got up and ran bath water. To my surprise, I didn't put any bubbles or scents in the water. As I put one foot in the water, a sense of panic came over me again.

Grabbing the Bible and re-reading the passage, I eased down into the water.

Once completely submerged in the tub, a peaceful calm came over me.

I began to fade back into time. Captivated in the capsule of time, my mind floated back to Memorial Day in 1999:

"Man it is hot as H* out here!" I thought as I stood in the front yard under the scantily leafed tree.

I was leaning on it thinking it was almost dead, but, like me, it lives on in spite of how fragile it may look.

Looks are not only deceiving, but disguising too.

The tree and I both hide what lies beneath the surface.

239

The tree had strong roots that totally deceived the eye of man because of the way it appeared—dry, rotted, and barely living.

My looks are disguising because I smile and appear perfect in every way, but on the inside I am a fragile shell of a person.

I guess this is why I would always find myself standing or sitting underneath this tree that provides a limited amount of shade from the onset of the brutal summer just around the corner.

As I stood there, I heard the door open. Looking up, I was thinking one of my sons was coming to interrupt my day-dreaming. Utterly surprised, I saw my stepfather coming towards me.

I instantly became angry, thinking, *"What the H* does he want?"*

It's bad enough Memorial Day celebration ended up being at my house, which happened to fall on my birthday; he's here, and now he comes outside while I'm trying to escape his face for a few moments.

My attitude went from cucumber cool to burnt fish-grease hot!

Can this day get any worse?

As I started to walk off, he said, "Granny Goose (his nickname for me), can I talk to you?"

I was baffled because as far back as I could recall, he never asked to talk to me with such a serious look.

I shrugged my shoulder, hoping he would take that as a "No," but he didn't.

"It's really important," he said.

"This better be good," I thought. Agitated, I said, "Go ahead and talk; I'm listening."

241

He started to sweat like he had run ten miles. "This is hard for me to ask, because in all these years, I have acted like I did nothing wrong."

"Oh, you did a lot wrong!"

"I know I did," he said. His eyes welled up with tears.

I could feel his pain. What? How could I start to feel sorry for this so-called man of God? He fondled me first; then full-out raped me, robbed me of all my innocence, and stole my trust in mankind.

Now I am standing here feeling sorry for him, and not myself.

"This is not fair by any means!" I thought to myself.

"Before you judge me, please know that I really am sorry for what I did to you. You did not deserve what I did."

"You mean I didn't deserve to be fondled or raped by you? You can't even say what you did. So how can you truly be sorry?"

"I am," he said as he held his head down. Tears were flowing like a faucet with a fast drip. "I can never change what I did, but I will do my best to show you that I am sorry. Words mean absolutely nothing without actions; I will spend the rest of my years showing you my remorse.

"Is there any way you can find it in your heart to forgive me?"

Forgive you? His question took me by surprise. I didn't know what to say. He stood there looking like a sad, lost dog. His eyes were bloodshot red. My mind was racing with emotions.

I guess he could see the hate and hurt in my eyes because he quickly said: "The Bible says, in order to be forgiven you must ask for forgiveness."

Standing there, I glared back at him, thinking he's got a lot of nerve to be asking for forgiveness years later.

I couldn't even answer him, because I was so mad; it was hot as H*; he looked like the Devil, and I was the fire surrounding him.

Beads of sweat started popping out on my forehead the way grease bubbles begin to boil up when you're deep frying catfish.

I didn't want to look at him standing there, as if he were the one violated.

I put my hand on my hip and said: "I guess so, since the Bible says forgiveness must be given to be forgiven."

Forgive! I wish I would, how could I forgive him? Last thing I remember is walking away from him saying, "I guess so since the Bible say to forgive."

Suddenly a knock on the bathroom door jarred me back into "REALITY."

"Who is it?"

"It's me, your baby boy, Mom; are you okay?"

"Yes baby, I'm okay. Give me a few minutes."

"Take your time. Simply making sure you are okay, because you have been in there for two hours."

"I have?"

"Yes, Ma'am."

He walked away before I could say anything else.

For the life of me, I could not understand why I thought about that day. Oh, well; I forgave him.

Well, that's what I thought; it wasn't until he was on his deathbed that I realized I hadn't really forgiven him.

He went into ICU on a Thursday. Not to mention he had been at the hospital for two weeks, and I still had not gone to see him.

I wanted him to suffer so badly. Everyone kept telling me I needed to get to the hospital. I found every excuse not to go.

Meanwhile, I was telling myself I had to get there because I did not want him to suffer. (At least that's the lie I was able to tell myself; feeling not one bit of guilt.)

A little bit of guilt came over me after attending church that Sunday. Pastor's Johnson's sermon topic was "Forgiveness is God's Way of Humbling You." The verse was 2 Chronicles 7:14: "If my people, which are called by my name, shall humble themselves, and pray, and seek my face, and turn from their wicked ways; then will I hear from heaven, and will forgive their sin, and will heal their land."

I was somewhat convicted.

Nonetheless, I still was not forgiving.

Trying to continue on in my normal fashion, I brushed Sunday's sermon off.

Monday and Tuesday seemed to fly past me. It was Wednesday—Bible study night didn't matter to me because I wasn't going. I planned to go to the movies instead.

Walking out the door heading to the movie theatre, my cellphone rang. I glanced at the number. *Sis. Johnson; hum, what could she possibly want?*

"Hello."

"Hi, Sharon, this is Sis. Johnson. How are you?"

"I am fine. How are you doing, Sis. Johnson?"

"I'm doing wonderful! I'm calling because tonight the Pastor is starting a series that I believe will help you grow more."

"Okay, but I will not be able to attend tonight; maybe next Wednesday."

"Sharon, I think you really need to attend tonight because the first lesson is the most important. If you miss tonight, it might be hard for you to understand later down the line."

"Sis. Johnson, I have other plans scheduled for this evening."

"Oh, okay; if you change your mind, we will be starting at seven instead of seven-thirty."

"Yes, Ma'am. Thank you for the information."

"You're welcome, be blessed. Bye now."

Finally at the theatre I got out with the car running. What! How could I have mixed up the movie show time? Darn it! The movies automated line said it started at six, not five fifteen. Shoot!

"Lord, it must be meant for me to attend Bible study," so I headed to the church.

I arrived early enough to sit down and enjoy watching the members mix and mingle, I saw Sis. Johnson, who looked like she'd been here before everyone, excuse herself from the members and come towards me with a friendly greeting and smile.

"I am so glad you made it, Sharon; you will be blessed tonight."

I politely smiled. "I certainly can stand a blessing."

"We all can."

I sat in my normal seat.

The congregation sung two hymns before Pastor Johnson entered the pulpit.

He prayed and then got right into Bible study.

"God has laid in my spirit to do a series on "Generational Curses."

"Um, this should be interesting."

"If you would turn your Bible to Exodus 34:7 KJV, it reads: "'Keeping mercy for thousands, forgiving iniquity and transgression and sin, and that will by no means clear the guilty; visiting the iniquity of the fathers upon the children and the children's children to the third and fourth generation."

The hair on the back of my neck stood up. *"Oh, my God!"* Sitting at full attention, I cleaved to the Pastor's every word. I took so many notes my hands cramped.

Once Bible study ended, Sis. Johnson came up to me, smiling.

I thought: *"What is she smiling so hard for?"*

"I hope this series will bring you all the answers you are seeking."

What? How could she know what is going on inside me? She quickly said: "Spiritual discernment is real." She hugged me, then turned to speak with others.

I couldn't wait to get home.

Driving home was a complete blur. I couldn't get over Pastor Johnson's lesson or Sis. Johnson's statement.

I completed the series and learned so much.

The most important thing I learned is when a generational curse has come upon a family, if no one calls it out, it continues.

Parents unknowingly help Satan keep the curses going from generation to generation because they raise their children the way they were raised, teaching the same principles they were taught.

Example: If they were spanked as a child, they spank their children. If they were told not to repeat what was said in the house, their children are taught the same. If they went to the doctor/dentist regularly, they took their children to the doctor/dentist regularly. If they grew up taking a bath daily, then so did their children. I could go on and on, but hopefully you get the picture.

Parents at some point must learn that the world is changing. There was a point in time when what our parents taught us was good, but with the way the world is now, we must begin to teach our children differently from the way we were taught.

The reason is because Satan is so cunning and deceitful with his plan of keeping generational curses going. He skillfully makes you feel that if you don't teach what your parents taught you, then you are doing things wrong as a parent.

Due to my abuse, I taught my boys from the time that they could understand, that no one was to touch them in any way. I took the time out to teach them what I was not taught. I showed them appropriate discipline, touching, hugging, and ("TRUE") innocent kisses. I was determined that what happened to me would not happen to my children.

Satan was not going to have free reign in my household, because I taught my boys to let someone know when they were being mistreated. It didn't matter if it was me, their father, aunts, or uncles; tell someone. Once they were of age to understand sexual abuse, I shared my story of abuse with them, letting them know that the abusers are usually the closest person to them. Of course they were shocked to find out that their Papa was my abuser, but they needed to understand that an abuser does not look like what the world portrays an abuser to look like. They are normal, everyday people who are seemingly the pillars of the community.

Due to my openness and deviation from what I was taught, Satan's molestation curse was not passed on to my sons (If abuse had occurred, it was not because I did not teach them.), to my knowledge.

I also assured them to this day that if they came and told me that they were abused as a child by anyone, I would do everything in my power to this day to bring charges against whoever the accused may be. I would not sweep it under the rug, let sleeping dogs lie, or let the past be the past as I was taught. My children will have justice and know that I am with them 100%!

This is the only way Satan's generational curses will be broken off from my generation.

If you have not changed your way of teaching your children, then more likely than not Satan has the opportunity to keep the generational curse ongoing in your family.

Exposing family secrets is the only way to break the cycle of generational curses.

Therefore, those who are not exposed to sicknesses in the family more than likely will fall victim to the generational curse.

They will not understand why they are doing what they have done, because the sicknesses remain hidden from them.

I instantly thought about my stepfather, remembering when my mother told me about his father doing the same thing to his children.

I began to understand the vicious cycle of generational curses and the hidden pains in my stepfather's eyes. It was the same pains I had hid in my eyes and my heart. The hidden pains of why me? What did I do to deserve this? How could I let this happen?

I wept for him, believing in my heart that he was a victim at some point, too.

This didn't excuse his behavior, but it certainly helped me truly forgive him, the day he died.

I was finally able to heal and let go of all the pain.

I will never forget the scars, but the pain; I have been delivered and freed.

Forgiveness is not easily done. However, if you sincerely seek God's help, it will come in time.

Remember, when you are unwilling to forgive, you will never be free of pain.

Forgiveness is an instant eye-opener, the perfect antidote to cure the pain of the past, present, and future.

I am a living witness to the power of true forgiveness. Although my abuser is dead and gone, the day before he died comes to mind; I woke up feeling a sense of depression I had never felt before. I was sad, deep within. *"God, what is this?"* I asked.

Suddenly, a sense of urgency came over me to get to the hospital. I knew I needed to let my stepfather know that I truly forgave him, as well as have his forgiveness for intentionally wanting him to suffer. Without second guessing my thoughts, I quickly got dressed to go to the hospital. I got outside to my car and could not believe the tire on the driver's side was flat, "Dang it!" Determined to get to the hospital, I ran back in the house and grabbed my friend's keys to his truck. In complete disbelief, his tire was flat in the back on the driver's side. Panic set in; I was an emotional wreck! I ran back into the house and asked him to help me change my tire. When we opened the trunk of my car to get the spare out, it was flat. I looked at him and he saw the panic in my eyes and he said: "Don't worry I'll change my tire."

"Ok."

We opened his trunk and took the jack and spare out, but could not find the lug nut wrench to unscrew his tire lugs. Thinking quickly, I remembered I had a four-way lug wrench (a wrench shaped like an X with different lug sizes). I ran into the garage, grabbed it, and took it to him. He placed the size he needed for his tire lug on the lug nut and tried to unscrew it, but could not get it loose. He tried with all his might. He turned to me and said, "They put the bolt on with an air gun and it is too tight for me to loosen. It will have to be towed to a tire shop for them to take off the tire."

"What! Are you saying I'm going to have to wait for a tow truck?" I said frantically.

"Yes, if you are going to drive it."

"Oh my God, what am I going to do? I can't wait that long." I was panicking and pacing back and forth.

"Hey it's going to be okay. Calm down Sweetheart," he said as he began to wipe away the tears coming down my cheeks. "Do you have a friend who might be able to take you to the hospital?" he asked, tenderly.

"No." I said as the tears in my eyes began to well up again.

"I can pay for you a taxi," he said excitedly.

"That's going to take too long. He will be dead before I get there. I have to get there now!"

I could clearly hear the loudness of panic and anger in my voice. If I had any doubt about my tone, it was clear that I was correct because when I looked at him he looked defeated and solution-less. I wanted to let him know I appreciated his kindness, so I said, "Thanks for trying."

"You're welcome," he replied as he went back inside.

Desperate to get to the hospital, I had to think and think quickly. I prayed: *"Lord, I know I need closure and his forgiveness for my wanting him to suffer. Will you please help me?"*

Suddenly, it came to me to call my client who had foot surgery; since the surgery she had not been using her car. I grabbed my cell phone and called her.

"Hello, Lynetta"; before I could say my name she said: "Hey Lady! What's up?"

"I need a huge favor."

"Okay."

"I need to use your car to get to the hospital. My step-father is expected to die any minute now, and I need to get there."

"Sure, you can use it. The only problem is I can't drive because of my foot."

"I know. Is it okay if I have someone bring me there?"

"Of course, that will be fine."

"Okay and thanks, Lynetta."

"You're welcome anytime."

I walked up the street to my neighbor's house and asked her to take me to Lynetta's house, and she did without hesitation.

"Thank you, Lord!" I uttered.

I got to the hospital. I rushed to his bedside and was shocked at the image of him. He was so tiny. His face was sunken in because his weight loss and his false teeth were out. (He looked like a monster that had been defeated after a hard fought battle.) As I got closer to him, I got scared. I turned to my sister, crying and shaking my head back and forth, saying: "I don't want to see him like that." He looked like he was barely hanging on. I knew in my heart that he was hanging on, waiting to see me. (I felt terrible for my heartlessness as I looked at a half-fraction of the man I knew.) I needed his forgiveness for not coming sooner. As soon as I got close enough for him to hear my voice, he began to try to mumble. (Everyone looked shocked because for days he'd laid motionless.) I leaned over, touched his forehead which was ice cold, and said: "its okay, I forgive you and thank you for waiting on me; forgive me for not coming sooner. You can go now."

He reached up and touched my hand, mumbling. In my heart for the first time I felt our sincerity. I turned to my family and said: *"He will go now."*

They all looked at me as if I was crazy, but I knew he had no more strength in him. He used what little he had left, waiting for me to get there.

As I left the room, the heaviness I felt before was gone. I felt light as a feather floating in the wind. I was free!

The next day he peacefully died.

"Thank you Lord, for giving me the opportunity to know that: "Forgiveness is Freedom from Fear and Faith in You Forever! Amen."

Closing thought.

When God is allowed to turn darkness into light, Satan has no power, and forgiveness comes easier, due to faith and trust in Him. See Acts 26:18 KJV, where Apostle Paul received his calling from Jesus: ("To open their eyes, and to turn them from darkness to light, and from the power of Satan unto God, that they may receive **forgiveness** of sins, and inheritance among them which are sanctified by faith that is in me.").

Conclusion

Am I My Brother's/Sister's Keeper?

"*Wow!*" I can't believe it has been nearly eight years since I started writing this book, and I am finally able to write the conclusion.

Chuckling with a smile on my face, I can proudly write this final chapter to "The Reality of Abuse, the Aftermath, and the Recovery."

After all my up's and down's from "The Reality of Abuse," "the Aftermath" of all my love and hate relationships, catapulted me to "the Recovery" through trial and error.

The "REALITY" of it all showed me that if it had not been for those who loved me conditionally or unconditionally, I would not have experiences to share. Thank you, whether you played a major or minor role in the Clay (Me) that the Potter (God) molded back together.

Because of His mercy and grace, I can truly say I understand, no matter what age I began to face the challenges of life, someone kept me through prayer, a kind word, or a simple smile.

As you read this finally chapter, may you feel the love that comes from within me for all people.

No matter the race, gender, political party, or religious belief of a person, we are all created by God and for His purpose. Although life's circumstances take us through different trials and tribulations, God will have the Glory and His revealing light will shine through us all.

Let us put aside our differences and try to live harmoniously in this world of imperfection. No man is perfect; we all have issues (seen or unseen), fears, hurts, hang-ups and bad habits. Regardless of how one may live their life, God is the only true judge at the end of one's lifetime journey.

After you have read the last word of this chapter, it is my prayer that through my discovery of being "My Brother's/ Sister's Keeper" you will perhaps become a keeper of someone.

"Relate, Rejuvenate, and Rejoice!"

My discovery begins:

I was sitting down, watching Judge Judy on TV, and my phone rang. *"This had better be good. Everybody knows when Judge Judy is on, I'm off, especially if I don't have a client."*

I looked at my phone and saw it was Shay. I know she was watching Judge Judy too and calling so we could laugh at the plaintiff, who was clearly being made a fool out of by Judge Judy.

"Hey Shay, what's up?"

"Girl, turn to CNN! Hurry up; you have got to see this craziness."

"Why? What is going on?"

"Have you turned onto CNN yet?"

"I'm changing the channel now."

"Sharon, say something!"

I stared at the T.V. horrified! I could not believe another young black man had been shot and killed by a white police officer.

"Shay, this cannot be happening again. We are still trying to get past the Trayvon Martin disaster!"

"I know. This is way too much, Sharon! These white people are out of control!"

"No, Ma'am; the world is out of control! Not just white people; ALL people, Shay."

"Girl, I know you are not getting ready to try to make an excuse for this, too?"

"No excuses, just 'REALITY.' God is so tired of everyone worrying about color in America. We need to leave race out and realize we are killing another American, and young ones at that!"

"Girl, these white folks don't care about that! All they care about is keeping a black person down, especially our black men."

"Shay, don't get me started."

"No Sharon, go ahead; I want to hear how you are going to try and make this right."

"I'm not trying to make anything be right; I just want people to be realistic."

"Realistic! Girl, how much more real can it get, shooting a young black man over a cigar? You do realize he was shot to death, right?"

"Shay, I hear as well as see it all. I just have a difference of opinion regarding these situations."

"I don't see how you can see it differently, because it is what it is!"

"No, Shay, it is what people want it to be; a black-and-white issue."

"Well it is!" Shay said drastically.

"Yes, in color it is, but in 'REALITY,' it is another way for Satan to win," I said calmly, because I knew Shay would start cussing like a sailor if she detected any other tone in my voice.

"Girl, what the H* does Satan have to do with this?"

"Everything—especially when it comes to the most blessed country in the world.

"Hello?"

"Yeah, I'm still here. Just listening, waiting for you to make sense."

"I can't believe you can't see how Satan is manipulating America into a chaos by using money, race, drugs, violence, and sex," I said.

"No, Sharon, I can't; please break it down to me."

"Hold on; let me read it to you straight from the Bible."

"Sharon, I don't want to have Bible study; I want answers."

"You see, Shay, that's the problem; too many people who profess to be a Christian, don't want to study the Bible or live it; just quote it!

"That's the real problem with not only America, but the world.

"No one wants to believe or use the only Book, to my knowledge, that can explain the chaos and shedding of innocent blood.

"Proverbs 6:12–15 KJV reads: '12A naughty person, a wicked man, walketh with a froward mouth. 13 He winketh with his eyes, he speaketh with his feet, he teacheth with his fingers; 14 Frowardness is in his heart, he deviseth mischief continually; he soweth discord. 15 Therefore shall his calamity come suddenly; suddenly shall he be broken without remedy.'

"Does this not describe what is happening with people in America right now?

"Are you there?" I asked.

271

"Yeah, I'm here," she replied softly.

Since she was quiet as a thief, I kept talking. "Americans don't think of the consequences of their actions. I know there is a lot going on in other countries, but I can only speak on America where I live.

"Most Americans wake up today thinking about getting ahead of the next person, without considering God. Whether they use their mouth, feet, hands, or fingers, it does not matter as long as they get ahead, with "NO" concern for the innocent people around them. People make wrong to be right and right to be wrong every chance they get, especially the so-called Christians.

"Michael Brown had taken something that was not his, and beat up an innocent -man; unfortunately, his lapse in judgment and his actions cost him his life.

"I am not saying the officer should have killed him, but what I am saying is this: put the blame where it belongs.

Michael Brown had no business stealing or beating on an innocent man doing his job.

"I know there have been problems with racism in Ferguson, but that still does not excuse his behavior."

"So you're saying this gave the police officer the right to kill him?"

"Yes. When you break the law and use violence while doing so, you place yourself in a situation of life or death. Think about it, Shay, officers' deal with criminals who have no regard for their own life and definitely not for the life of the one coming to prevent them from whatever it is they are trying to achieve. Now, this officer gets a call saying an armed robbery has taken place, and the suspect beat the victim with a weapon and has fled the scene. He is a black male, wearing a gray hoodie, about six feet tall.

"Um huh," Shay mumbled.

"Keep in mind the officer could have just left a similar crime scene and was not able to save the victim, barely escaping with his own life. "Do you not think he is going to protect himself when coming face-to-face with another crime that has the same similarities as the crime scene he just left?" Better yet, put yourself in this officer's place. What would you do?"

"Well, I ain't Jesus, and you know me well enough to know that if someone's coming at me wrong after I just got through getting into it with someone else, the fight would be on, and Jesus would be the only one to save them from me," Shay said. We both laughed so hard because what she said was so true.

"Seriously, this could be exactly what happened in this unfortunate situation. Boycotting and rioting are not the remedy to these terrible circumstances."

Before I could say anything, Shay blurted out, "Why not, Sharon? It worked for Dr. King."

"Come on now, Shay, surely you have got to be kidding me. We live in a different day and time.

"Besides, when Dr. King fought, he did not believe in violence, just freedom for all. I know he has to be in Heaven looking down, appalled at the way blacks handle unfair situations today.

"Just look at the T.V. Blacks are destroying where they live. What sense does that make, Shay?"

"Now I agree with you totally about the way they are tearing up their own neighborhoods."

"I'm glad you can at least see my point."

Shay yawns.

"Shay, are you ready to get off the phone?"

"I do have the late shift tonight."

"Okay let me make my final point: If Americans are so concerned about racial violence, why not send black officers to the scene when dealing with a black offender? I guarantee you, Satan would not be able to continually keep the news cluttered with racism."

"Now you talkin', Sharon; that's something they should consider. Although it might be a little hard to do, it's worth a try."

"Shay, until Americans get some sense, we the true believers must come together, and pray that God will fix our hearts to have compassion instead of our passions."

"What do you mean by 'compassion instead of our passions'?"

"Michael handled the situation with his passion for a cigar, and the police officer had no compassion for a young American when he shot Michael.

"To sum it up in a nut shell, 'REALITY' shows that Michael should not have been stealing, and the police officer should have used his Taser gun instead of his glock."

"Sharon, I don't know how you do it, but what you said does make a lot of sense. You get on my last nerve sometimes because you always make me think from a whole different perspective, even when I don't want to. I love you, girl, and I will talk to you later."

"I love you more for at least listening to me, because most won't even hear me.

"Thanks, Shay, for being my friend to the end!"

She laughed, but before she could hang up, I said, "It never ceased to amaze me when it comes to sports or any competing event against another country, every American 'comes proudly together; no one cares about the color of the American as long as he or she is American."

"Speak on, sista, but I got to go! Love ya bunches."

All I heard was silence. I laughed because she hung up so fast, as if to say, "That's all!"

As I continued to watch the violence erupt, I started thinking of my own son who did the same thing; only he used a weapon.

I made no excuses for what he did. When the police came to my house with their hands on their guns surrounding me, I knew my son was in big trouble, and if they got to him first, the probability of him being shot or killed was too risky for me to not try to find him first.

Especially after talking with the detective and looking at all the officers surrounding me, my maternal radar went on high alert, sensing the level of danger my son had placed upon himself.

My only prayer was, "Lord let me get to him before they do."

Once I saw my son, I said: *"Thank you Lord, for allowing me to get to him first."*

Continuing to watch the reporting on Michael Brown, I said a quick prayer for his family, asking God to give them strength to deal with their loss, and to help Americans realize we must come together as a united country.

Our pledge is "United we stand; divided we fall"; we are falling, America!

All the vicious acts of violence are the motivating factors behind this final chapter: "Am I My Brother's/ Sister's Keeper?"

YES I AM!

How do I know this?

I read it for myself in Ecclesiastes 4:9–12 KJV: 9 "Two are better than one; because they have a good reward for their labour. 10 For if they fall, the one will lift up his fellow: but woe to him that is alone when he falleth; for he hath not another to help him up. [11] Again, if two lie together, then they have heat: but how can one be warm alone? [12] And if one prevail against him, two shall withstand him; and a threefold cord is not quickly broken." It plainly says two can do better than one.

Not only does the Bible say it, but life has proven that two heads are better than one.

Take for example, when you have a problem too big for you to solve by yourself, did you not seek the advice of someone else?

When your hands are full, and you can't open the door for yourself, someone else opens the door for you.

When you are sick and unable to get well, you go to the doctor.

Let' go back even further. When you were born, someone had to teach you how to do everything.

Therefore, I ask again, "Am I My Brother's/Sister's Keeper?" "YES I AM!"

If God did not intend for us to keep one another, then why did He create so many people with different abilities?

Although there are some who use their abilities in the wrong way, God still created them. They just choose to do things the way they want.

It never ceases to amaze me how those who use their talents to do wrong stick together.

Example: Gang members will lay down their lives for each other.

Dope dealers will only sell to those who use drugs or wish to sell them.

However, the most important thing that I have learned from these individuals who stick together is that they do not excuse behavior that is not in conjunction with what they believe.

Example: If you cross one gang member, you've crossed all members, and you will be taken care of according to their rules.

If you cross a dope dealer, you will be dealt with according to the rules of their world.

Sitting back and being observant, I have discovered the problem with most Christians: "EVERYTHING IS EXCUSABLE.".

Example: If fellow Christians are doing something that is not of God, and you try to tell them that it is not right, the first thing they do is excuse their behavior by quoting to you: "Judge not, that ye not be judged" (Matt.7:1 KJV), quickly making you feel like a hypocrite.

But they never go past that Scripture (to the next verses), because if they did, they would not continue to use it to excuse their ungodly behavior.

The reason is that, reading past the first verse, you will find that you are not being a hypocrite as long as you have gotten the beam out of your own eye; then you can tell your "Christian brethren" what they are doing wrong. (Matthew 7:5 KJV: "Thou hypocrite, first cast out the beam out of thine own eye; and then shalt thou see clearly to cast out the mote out of thy brother's eye.").

Notice, I said your "Christian brethren"; you cannot go tell a sinner that he or she is wrong, because they will turn around and attack you, since they have NO relationship with God, nor do they want one (yet). (Matthew 7:6 KJV: "Give not that which is holy unto the dogs, neither cast ye your pearls before swine, lest they trample them under their feet, and turn again and rend you.")

283

If you are not talking to a fellow Christian, don't waste your time.

You will know if they are a true believer, because you as a believer should know the tree by the fruit it produces. (Matthew12:33 KJV: "Either make the tree good, and his fruit good; or else make the tree corrupt, and his fruit corrupt: for the tree is known by his fruit.")

I'm not saying a Christian should not try to help a sinner to Christ; I am saying, make sure you are led by Christ when dealing with those who do not know Christ.

If you are not led by the Holy Spirit, you will soon be made to look foolish and not wise because of vain confidence. (Proverbs 14:16 KJV: "A wise man feareth, and departeth from evil: but the fool rageth, and is confident.")

For Christians who are truly trying to be your "Christian" brother's keeper, when correcting them, let them know you are not judging them; you are merely speaking about what you see. (See Matthew 12:33 KJV, above.)

However, if your fellow "Christian" brother or sister is in judgment, have no worries, God will shut them up! (Psalms 31:18 KJV: "Let the lying lips be put to silence; which speak grievous things proudly and contemptuously against the righteous.")

Listen up, Christians! It is time for us to start holding each other accountable.

How can Christians expect to change the world when the church of God is so much like the world?

Christians cannot expect changes in the church until they stop accepting the things of the world into the church. (1 John 2:15–17 KJV: 15 "Love not the world, neither the things that are in the world. If any man love the world, the love of the Father is not in him. 16 For all that is in the world, the lust of the flesh, and the lust of the eyes, and the pride of life, is not of the Father, but is of the world. [17] And the world passeth away, and the lust thereof: but he that doeth the will of God abideth for ever.")

Example: Praise dancing. It is wonderful to give praises unto God through dance, but when do Christians stop and say enough? Some songs that are meant to give "God the Glory," are misleading. People of the church (Christians) and the world (SINNERS) are left confused after hearing the music. Christians don't know whether they should give praises to God or dance. Sinners know to dance and give no praises to God.

What a mess! Who's converting who? From the looks of things, the world is converting the church, instead of the church converting the world.

I know many will not agree with me, but look at the church: politics is now part of the church, misleading music causes some dancing that should not be in the church, rap music is in the church, openly gay relationships are in the church, and heads of churches have affairs with men, women, boys, and girls; the list of how the world is converting the church can go on, but I'll stop right here.

Why is the church looking so much like the world? It's because excuses are made for everything going on within the church.

Many believe the church is where all the sinfulness can be fixed.

News flash: if a sinner does not want to be fixed, the church is not the place for the sinner.

The "Bible" (not what I say, but the Bible) says that these people should be put out of the church to let God deal with them. (1 Corinthians 5:11–13 KJV: 11 "But now I have written unto you not to keep company, if any man that is called a brother be a fornicator, or covetous, or an idolator, or a railer, or a drunkard, or an extortioner; with such an one no not to eat. 12 For what have I to do to judge them also that are without? Do not ye judge them that are within? 13 But them that are without God judgeth. Therefore put away from among yourselves that wicked person."; 2 Corinthians 6:13–14 KJV: "13 Now for a recompence in the same, (I speak as unto my children,) be ye also enlarged. 14 Be ye not unequally yoked together with unbelievers: for what fellowship hath righteousness with unrighteousness? and what communion hath light with darkness?")

Before I continue and close this chapter, let me say to you that no matter where you are in your walk of life, I am not here to judge you. I am simply saying that we as brothers and sisters in Christ must find a way to not only fellowship and pray together, but we must hold one another accountable for our actions when representing Christ.

In closing, I leave you with this, my brothers and sisters in Christ: Ecclesiastes 3:1–8KJV: "To everything there is a season, and a time to every purpose under the heaven: 2 A time to be born, and a time to die; a time to plant, and a time to pluck up that which is planted; 3 A time to kill, and a time to heal; a time to break down, and a time to build up; 4 A time to weep, and a time to laugh; a time to mourn, and a time to dance; 5 A time to cast away stones, and a time to gather stones together; a time to embrace, and a time to refrain from embracing; 6 A time to get, and a time to lose; a time to keep, and a time to cast away; 7 A time to rend, and a time to sew; a time to keep silence, and a time to speak; 8 A time to love, and a time to hate; a time of war, and a time of peace".

This passage helped me realize for years, in spite of all the painful circumstances I faced or continue to face, I was at some point and will always be in time, a keeper of my brothers and sisters in Christ.

If you feel you are not your brother's or sister's keeper, I ask you to read this chapter as many times as you need to in order to understand and accept that regardless of the pain you may feel towards someone, in "TIME" you have to let it go in order to move forward. Once you accept this "REALITY," ask yourself this question: *"Am I My Brother's/Sister's keeper?"* According to the above passage, "YOU ARE YOUR BROTHERS/SISTERS KEEPER!"

If you still find it impossible to believe that you can be a keeper of a brother or sister in Christ who has wronged you, count the number of times the word *time* is used in the passage, and you will know without any doubt that in "TIME" all things are possible. But don't wait too long, or time will run out for you to forgive them (I was blessed that time did not run out for me). You don't want God to refrain from forgiving you because you did not forgive them do you?

May the light of God continue to radiate through all who believe there is a "TIME" for everything. Thanks for reading and please, my brothers and sisters in Christ, keep being my keeper!

www.ingramcontent.com/pod-product-compliance
Lightning Source LLC
Chambersburg PA
CBHW060007100426
42740CB00010B/1423